FOREGONE
Know Thyself

FOREGONE

ISBN 979 8 41974 193 5

Huge thanks to everyone who helped shape the person that is today
Dante Sapatinas.

FOREGONE

TABLE OF CONTENTS

FOREGONE

DISCLAIMER

This book is not meant to replace the advice of a doctor, a lawyer, a parent, a therapist, or anyone else, qualified or unqualified. As we grow up and we deal with situations, some things are better left to professionals, as advice given in the right time by the right person can change a person's life for the better.

Thus, I state now that I am not to be held responsible for getting yourself into trouble as a result of following these lessons & rules. Although I try to write as clear as I can, and to explain what the chapter is about with the last paragraph of the chapter, *What to take away,* a message can still be misinterpreted. I like to think that I also make it clear from the title of a chapter what the message is. Regardless of my two contingency plans, always make sure to research that which you do not understand, instead of acting on impulse. To check another's opinion about what you don't understand, instead of declaring it your new law. More about the disclaimer at the end of the book.

FOREGONE

CONTENT

In order to remove suffering you must be noble. What is suffering, if not the sum of our choices? And even if we shift the blame on another, are we not to blame for letting another ruin us? Are emotions not born of our judgement, and therefore an extension of us? So how can another ruin our lives and bring us suffering if we do not let them?

The first step to remove suffering from our life is to realise that it is a result of our choices. The second step to remove suffering from our life is to realise that our choices can also bring peace, but only by categorising and separating the good from the bad. By discovering the bad in our lives, and by removing it.

In order to respect another, we must first respect ourselves, for we cannot be good if we do not understand what it means to be good. We cannot exercise justice in our life if we are not prudent, and if we are not prudent we cannot respect another, for we don't know how.

What is bravery, if not the acceptance of fear and the conquering of it? Bravery is the soul determining that what we stand for is right, in spite of the fear of the unknown we feel. Bravery is the action of pursuing what we proposed on doing in the first place, regardless of the fear we feel.

Chapter IIII | *page 44*
TEMPERANCE

Lack of self-control is the mother of most problems, be it physical or mental. Just like medicine can cure, it also kills in high doses. Just like food feeds us, it also give us diabetes in high doses. Just like anger is a weapon to be mastered, unmastered it is a weapon to be used against us by others. Control is exercised in accordance with reason. *Ceteris Paribus* (Latin for 'all things should remain equal').

Chapter V | *page 50*
THE ROOM

What's the fastest way to make the world better? Fear. What's the best way to make the world better? Love, and first we must love ourselves. We love ourselves by being noble, by being prudent, just, brave, and tempered. By taking the right choices, by looking around us and putting in order that which is not in order. By making good out of bad.

Chapter Ω | *page 60*
KNOW WHO YOU ARE

We are our ego, and our ego is a library of information that works even in the absence of prudence. Although beneficial until a certain point, we need to dissolve the ego in order to become 'who we want to become', which is a person free of suffering. A noble person.

Chapter 1A | *page 66*
FOCUS ON WHAT YOU CAN CONTROL

Step one of dissolving our ego is to question what choices we have. Since the only thing we have control over is our choices, we start there.

After understanding that we have control over our mind only, and therefore our choices, we then start to question our actions. We categorise our behaviour through prudence in good and bad, and we gain deeper understanding of the faults in judgement we are susceptible to.

Next, we understand that our anger is a weapon to be mastered. Either by us for ourselves, or by others against us. To be virtuous isn't to allow evil into your life without fighting back, but to be capable of evil and to choose not to inflict it. Is everything you feel not a result of your mind, and if so, is your mind not within your ability to control?

We must further develop our understanding of life & reality (as will be seen in the *Prologue* chapter). What we feel, hear, and see isn't reality until proven so through evidence. Alike a test where we double-verify our answers before we submit, so too must we gather information and verify whether our senses do not mislead us. Whether what we see is not what it actually is, but what we want to see.

Nobody likes their rights being taken from them, and so don't take others' rights from them. Stand bravely by your rights, and know that to be brave and tempered is a result of being prudent and just. To be aggressive or passive is none of those, but to be assertive is all of them.

and the detriments of negative-nervous-system-stressing-behaviours, such as drinking, bad diet, bad sleep, smoking, lack of exercise, etc.

Chapter 2 | *page 160*
HAPPINESS IS THE JOURNEY, NOT THE DESTINATION

Chemically speaking, the best way to activate happiness is by making a plan. A part of our brain deals with executive functions, and activation of this part leads to activation of the happiness chemical. Once we understand this, we move to the next section.

Chapter 3 | *page 166*
THE CREATIVE PROCESS

Discovering and planning! Here we shall discover what our soul's purpose is through one simple exercise: using one hour of our time every day to implement *the creative process*! This process will show us what we feel attracted to long after our excitement wore off, and start our journey!

Chapter 4 | *page 174*
THE PRINCIPLE OF THE QUESTION 'WHY?'

People are lazy sometimes. How many times have we skipped work and ordered fast-food when we should've been working and cooking instead? Just because we know what we need to do doesn't mean that we will do it. That is why it is important to have a strong answer to the question 'why?'.

Chapter 5A | *page 182*
STOP LYING TO YOURSELF

After understanding what you want to do for the rest of your life, and why you want to do it, it is now important to look around you and address those activities that you know to be wasting your time, and therefore your potential.

As soon as you look around you and realise that some activities lead to 'who you want to be', and some do not, it is time to make a plan/schedule for the day. It is time to add the most important activities to the beginning of your day, and leave pleasures at the end of it. Think about a cheque: you save, and then you spend, not the other way around.

Instead of looking at the top of the mountain, which is daunting, we will make another plan, but this time it will cover more than a day. This plan will have short-term, medium-term, and long-term goals, and its purpose is to remind us that our choices are only exercised in the present, and that who we are today is a result of the choices of yesterday. So the thing we need to do is realise that we need to reach the top, but only by looking at the two steps in front of us, and believing in our strength to reach the top of the mountain!

Comparing is a sensitive subject, but in my opinion it is sometimes necessary. However, we must define the way we compare in order to not fall in a sad state. Thus, we must compare ourselves to ourselves for health benefits, and with others for competitive sportsmanship. There's no reason to be healthier than another, but to be healthier than your past-self? All the reasons.

AUTHOR'S NOTE

Dante Sapatinas
(26th of January 1994)

WHO: That is a really good question. I don't have a lot to say about myself: I joke an unhealthy amount of times per minute, I talk a lot, I try to learn from my mistakes, I like reading, I love drawing, I love going to the gym, and I love the summer. The only things I want in life is to be healthy, and to help as many people as I can. That's the best description I can come up with about myself.

WHAT: This book teaches the lessons and the rules I learned, and talks about the steps I took to fix my life. These lessons were learned from the great minds of the old masters, such as Socrates, Chrysippus, Diogenes, Seneca, Epictetus, Marcus Aurelius, etc., and the new masters, such as Mr. Jordan B. Peterson.

The story begins with the miracle of an epiphany that happened when I was around 24 years old: I found my character's biggest flaw, *'assuming'*. I put some research in it and my life changed. Years of unjustified anger and spontaneous combustion went out the window. I looked in the mirror and realised the kind of weirdo I have been my whole life, and how people took advantage of that. Fast forward a year, and my relationships improved, my overall look on life improved, and my mental health was (and is) amazing. But what changed? Surely this small step I've implemented where *I no longer assume the reason behind anything, but instead question and patiently try to understand without prejudice* couldn't have been the catalyst that led to the bettering of my life, could it? In fact, it could. It was.

You see, in not assuming you find truth and freedom. The truth that, in general, *you don't have any real knowledge about anything in life, only prejudice that is born of your perception*, and the freedom born from the realisation that *you no longer must be a prisoner of your prejudice since you can always learn the reality of something by questioning and understanding it.* Fear not though, for we won't talk only about assuming, but about many other lessons that are so important, no amount of italicizing, boldening, or underlining can emphasise their invaluable meaning.

I address this book to all who struggle in life. To all who are well-intended. To all who cannot pinpoint the exact thing in their behaviour that makes them an 'outsider'. I address this book to myself. I am a man that somehow got through life until the age of 24 with nothing but ignorance. I would have continued to be ignorant if I didn't have the privilege to move to London, Great Britain, the privilege to be exposed to a different culture. I have been interested in understanding and documenting human behaviour ever since I had that aforementioned epiphany, and although I started writing at 26, I realised only recently what I want to say with this book: that there is only one *true* way of living life peacefully, and that is by being noble!

As a kid I wouldn't have searched for a book on this topic, obviously, but now I realise the importance of teaching a young one these lessons. I realise how better my life would have been if I knew about these rules, and how it is my duty to pass them on to future generations so that they have a better life than I did, or hope they do. You see, recently I went back to my country and I noticed that people haven't changed. Everyone is still acting entitled and spoiled, topics like inter-social behaviour, empathy, and personal development are still absent. The reason is because barbarity is still the answer, not benevolence.

Thus, I feel it is my moral obligation to try and bring the world up to speed on these lessons that will not only develop us as better human beings, but also help us develop better as social beings, and maybe even as better parents and kids too!

INTRODUCTION

I would like to open the book by mentioning the utmost important lesson since my creation. This is a lesson of the soul, and it is the foundation of this book: know that life showed me how *an 'evil' action can stem from a good intention*, and how *a bad day can be seen as good* from a different perspective. That everything is rooted in our perception, to be brief.

Aside from the obvious capital evil actions (such as killing, torturing, raping, abducting, etc.), please note that life is not necessarily white or black, and terms such as good and evil are only created by our logic. Life is made of grey colour that can turn either white or black, depending on where we stand. The woman that is 'evil' for stealing bread is good for feeding her baby. The parent that is 'evil' for taking the misbehaving child's phone away is good for personal development.

The subject of this book is 'how to remove suffering, instil peace, and find happiness in your life', and it is based (not entirely) on my understanding of the school of Stoicism:

- In section 1, *'WHO AREN'T YOU?'*, I will bring in discussion the term 'nobility', what it represents, what it consists of, and the importance of wanting (and aiming) to be noble every day. The purpose of this section is to explain to you that you aren't noble, and to show you why you aren't and how to become noble, eventually. I am no hero myself, do not worry. I too have behaviour that isn't noble, but I try to learn and redirect myself because nobility removes suffering, and brings peace.

- In section 2, *'WHO ARE YOU?'*, I will guide you to become noble. To be prudent, just, brave, and tempered. The purpose of this section is to bring you 'peace' and eliminate suffering. Briefly put, life's suffering stems from not knowing yourself, and that is a consequence of lacking control.

- In section 3, *'WHO DO YOU WANT TO BE?'*, I will guide you to discover the talent/passion that you want to pursue in life, and how to squeeze the most potential out of it. The purpose of this chapter is to bring you 'happiness'. It will cover topics like the creative process, motivation, addictions, not lying to yourself anymore, etc.

There will be several experiences selected from my personal life that will tackle certain obstacles and, although the experiences might seem specific and banal, *it is important to understand the mechanism behind them*, and not to focus on the banality of the example (see the chapter *Welcome your darkness*, for example). The reason behind that is because one day you might be facing a daunting situation which is fuelled by the mechanism presented, and you won't know how to confront it because you focused on looking at the tree, not at the forest itself. So don't look at my example, instead look at the message behind it, at the mechanism.

The purpose of this book is to improve your confidence, social interaction, mental health, and overall life. We often mistakenly think that mental health, unless diagnosed by a doctor as something visibly/palpably wrong, is otherwise fine. But mental health also relates to our daily stress, our impulses, how we respond to stimulus, our motivation to pursue our goal, etc.

The reason for writing this book has to do with a little joke of mine: I do not *have* a nervous system, *I am* a nervous system. Sometimes we erupt and lose our cool, we take irrational decisions in the heat of the moment, we assume when instead we should be asking, we normalize certain behaviours that should not be normalized…this must stop!

Your main mission in life is to confront every single situation with 'what can I learn from this?'. To gather wisdom. That is what this entire book is about.

PROLOGUE

What is life? How do you define life? Do you not define life from your own perspective? Do you not define life from the perception born of your perspective? Do you not define life from the perception you have based on your interpretation of sensory information (your senses), from what you feel, see, and hear? How do you know if your senses reflect the truth, that which is real? How do you define real? Withal, since two perspectives are usually different from one another, if you define life based on the evidence of your senses, and someone else defines life on the evidence of their senses, does that mean that their definition of life is wrong since you two have contradicting evidence?

My answer to that is no. I think that we each have a definition, and that all of them are correct since they are based on the interpretation of our senses. Thus, if we are suffering, we will believe that life is suffering, and if we are happy, we will believe that life is wonderful. There's no problem in questioning what life is and getting it wrong, because nothing stays the same. The problem appears when we confuse life with reality, when we question what reality is, and when we get it wrong.

What is reality? Reality is the defined and unchangeable state of things, devoid of our perception. Be that the laws of physics, or something like the state of a glass of water being full, regardless if we believe it to be empty.

Let's say you are in school, and today the teacher is giving a lesson about a glass of water. The teacher puts a full glass of water on the table, but because you're in the back and can't see well, you aren't sure if the glass is full or empty, *so you choose to believe it's empty*. Regardless of your perception of it, the glass is full. Why? Because your perception of it is based on the accumulated information from your senses, from what you saw and from what you believe, not on what the actual reality is: that the glass is full.

If the teacher asks something about the glass:

- The correct solution is to raise your hand and say that you can't see well, and that you'd like to know if the glass is full or empty before you answer the question, and only then to formulate your answer, accordingly.
- The wrong solution is to assume that, based on the information provided by your senses (which you believe to be sufficient), you have a good answer. Even if your answer would be right if the glass was empty, it is wrong since the glass is full. So you can apply the right behaviour to the wrong perception.

To explain why that is a wrong behaviour, think as if this was a math school test: you took the answers you provided as correct, without double verifying them, and consequently got a low grade. Wouldn't you punch yourself for not spending five more minutes on checking your answers before submitting, and thus ensuring that you get the maximum possible grade that you could get? It's not that you didn't know mathematics, it's that you didn't verify your answers before submitting them! A small + or – changes the entire equation!

So too happens in life. So too we look at something and, before questioning if that is the actual state of them (if what we see, think and believe about them is the actual reality or just our perception), we open our mouth and let go of words that we can't take back. It's not that we don't have the wisdom to know better, it's that we choose to not question and verify our words before we release them! + & -

But what makes us not submit our thoughts to a filter before we submit them? What makes us think that our perception is reality itself, and can we do anything to correct that? YES. WE. CAN, and this is what

I plan on doing with these three sections. I plan on opening your eyes to your choices, and to remove your suffering with some simple lessons!

I'm a weirdly constructed person, but in all honesty, I wouldn't want to be someone else. Based on this, I understand that each and every one of you that reads this book is also different. I understand that what works for some might not work for others, and I try to take that into account whenever I write a chapter. Regardless of how different we are from one another, at the end of the day we can all agree on this: suffering sucks, and we all wish for it to end!

To end things in high fashion, I am now going to say something controversial, and at surface it might seem contradictory to what I'm going to talk about in this book: I like being irrelevant. Or better said, I don't want to stay relevant for all of my life. I like being random, spontaneous, starting new activities, and although I'm full of energy and know my purpose, one day I'll stop being so energetic. One day I will want to settle down and enjoy every day however it comes at me. And if that day comes, I must understand early on that I can be *happy* and upright, or *sad* and hunched, regardless if I am relevant or not. Which one would you choose to be?

Having said all of that, I'd like to take a moment to thank you for your interest in this book. I hope that this is what you're looking for: the solution to your problems, the answer to your questions. I wish you a good read!

FOREGONE

WHO AREN'T YOU?

Chapter Nulla
THE APOCALYPSE OF NOBILITY

Everything can be taken from a man but one thing: the last of the human freedoms—to choose one's attitude in any given set of circumstances, to choose one's own way.
— VIKTOR FRANKL

WHO AREN'T YOU?

I want to open your mind to one simple question:

What will make people remember you?

I ask this because it has a purpose that is not evident. It is not a question you should answer, not immediately anyway. Instead, it is a question that should guide you to comprehend your behaviour. To think about what makes a person worth remembering, and to start working on being that person.

You don't decide to be good when people remember you. People remember you when you decide to be good.

But why? Because we like remembering the good times we had with good people, and detest remembering the bad times provoked by bad people. It's true that we learned and matured, but we still detest bad moments and bad people. Based on that, goodness is the thing people will remember you for.

If I am to be remembered for something in this life, I wish to be remembered for bringing Stoicism to the modern world, and connecting more people with it. Although founded in time immemorial (3rd century B.C.), the lessons this philosophical school teaches apply today still! These lessons are the fundamental traits required to improve your life and lessen your suffering, the traits that are yours to take if you so wish!

It is my opinion too that you should always pursue wisdom and virtue, as our Stoic forefathers put it, and the reason for that is to remove the suffering from your life. Engaging in bad behaviour brings misery, but engaging in good behaviour removes suffering!

NOBILITY

What is *nobility?* *Nobility* is the highest virtue, and it should be the trait we pursue in life every day. A virtue is a behaviour that shows high moral standards. When I will talk in this book about anything like 'being yourself', I do not mean that you should be rude if you are rude. I mean that you should:

- Question your behaviour (your recklessness, impatience, pride, wrath, etc.).
- Question what reasons you have behind doing what you do (what exactly in your behaviour makes you behave rudely. Who hurt you?).
- Question if this is who you want to be (furious, ashamed, disgraced, embarrassed, etc.).
- Question about *who you want to be* (gentle, modest, understanding).
- Aim to have a behaviour that leads to who you want to be, *and who you **should** want to be is someone who is noble!*

One very important bit of information I bring to attention before we begin our journey: this book is written with the purpose of trying to bring more nobility in your life, *and everything that we will talk about will stem from the assumption that you are aiming to be noble*, that you are aiming to respect the teachings of this book, even if you might not. Briefly put, when I say that you should 'know (and be) yourself', I mean that you should know yourself according to nobility, and that you should always strive to be noble, as being rude is not noble! Why? So you don't suffer anymore! Nobility brings peace thanks to the four cardinal virtues it consists of:

- Prudence is the mother of all virtues, and its purpose is to give us reason. It teaches us not only to define what is good (listening, understanding, helping) and what is bad (negligence, inconsistency, precipitance), but to also *act* good.
- Justice is not only the respect we show God and others, but it's also the acknowledging that all humans are equal. We demonstrate this virtue (that we are just) by treating everyone the same: fair, honest, equally. By being prudent.
- Fortitude is not the lack of fear, but the strength to push through it. It's an ability that is exercised with reason, it's the virtue that helps us achieve what we propose, that helps us get up when we are down.
- Temperance is the virtue that teaches us to abstain from overindulgence, from giving in to our desires, to our pleasures. It teaches us that every trait pushed to its extreme can devolve into a pathology. That which cures also kills in higher doses.

Thus, your behaviour must consist of the four cardinal virtues: you must be prudent, just, brave, and tempered, and when you reach that point you will realise that nothing can stand in your path! No amount of words, insults, or discouragement! You will realise that the only obstacle in this life is the fear you produce within your mind by focusing on the things you cannot control!

Now to address the baby elephant in the room, a common misbelief about the word apocalypse is that it represents 'the end' or 'pain and suffering', but that's not what it means. The word comes from the Greek language, from 'apokalypsis', which means revelation. It means to see something you couldn't see before, to uncover, to disclose. This chapter and its title has a double entendre, for I wish to both say that nobility has dimmed and looks like it's coming to an end in our day and age, and also unveil what nobility is, and why it is important to implement it in your daily life!

I plan to uncover nobility to your mind, to disclose it before your soul. I plan on opening your eyes to how not everything in life is what it seems to be, and how all the suffering in your life is a result of your choices. Daunting as that may seem, know that your choices can also remove the suffering from your life, and that the 'rules' and lessons I shall present in this book will not constrict you, but empower you!

Nobody likes rules. We are free spirited beings, some more than others, and thus we feel constricted by them. But the best rules do not take away freedom, instead they instil that behaviour which takes away suffering!

Nobody likes suffering. There's nothing there for us, and somehow we believe that an outside force keeps us in this loop of continuous suffering, when in reality it's only us and the choices we take that make us suffer. Suffering can be anything: despising the job we have, fighting with rude customers, not having anything in our lives that makes us happy, not having a purpose nor aim, not having the slightest idea how to start or where to go. Suffering has many forms, and the best thing we can do to start removing it from our lives is to realise that our suffering hasn't changed with the behaviour we have. If our current behaviour is the cure to eliminating suffering, then why are we still suffering? Withal, if nothing changes with the behaviour we have, then shouldn't we understand that we must change our behaviour in order to not suffer anymore? That in order to get peace, that which we've never had, we must do that which we never did?

BUT WHY?

St. Paul says that our thoughts should be directed to all that is true and deserves respect. All that is honest, pure, admirable, decent, worthy of praise, and virtuous (Philippians 4:8). But what does it mean to be virtuous, to be noble? What is nobility?

Nobility is the behaviour we adopt where we choose to seek what is good and what is bad, where we choose to differentiate between the two *in order to **act good***. Only knowing what is good and what is bad is not enough.

We can learn virtues from our parents as we grow up through the good reason they instil in us, but these are not enough for the suffering to stop. For the opinions of others to not hurt. For ungratefulness to end. Thus, we need to strengthen ourselves through deliberate education. I say deliberate education because we cannot learn that which we do not want to learn, and thus we must first understand why we'd want to change ourselves. Why we'd want to be noble!

'But how do we change ourselves?', you ask. Through wisdom. Through the wisdom of others. We must be grateful to our parents and remember how they picked us up when we fell, and in the same way look for help at those who are morally right, those who are regarded as the pedestals of wisdom, those who can help us get back up. The Old Testament says that anyone who loves righteousness will enjoy the fruits of her labour, which are temperance, prudence, justice, and courage, and nothing is more useful than these! (Wisdom 8:7).

This is no easy task, and you will be tested. As there are four stages of competence, you will go through four trials, each harder than the previous:

- **Unconscious incompetence (Ignorance):** That stage where not only will you not know what to do, how to do it, and why it is detrimental if you don't do it, but you will also deny the necessity and usefulness of the skill. You must question the necessity of nobility and come to the realisation on your own terms.
- **Conscious incompetence (Awareness):** That stage where, although you won't know how to start, you'll understand that you must start. You'll understand the detriments of not being noble, and you will understand the necessity and benefits nobility will bring to your life.
- **Conscious competence (Learning):** That stage where you will have researched the topic and understand how to do it. This is the stage where the skill of being noble is not perfected, it is not a habit, it is not a reflex, and thus concentration is required at this stage, but there is thought and action being put into the behaviour of acting noble.
- **Unconscious competence (Mastery):** That stage where you have 'mastered' the topic, where you have put at least 10,000 active hours (417 days) in it, where there has been daily practice and there still is

and will be. Where the skill is your second nature. Just as you can talk on the phone and execute your tasks, so too will you be out in the world and noble at the same time.

That is why it is important to not despair, for this is all a challenge, and after each stage you will be better, so what's there to despair about? *The secret in life is to focus on what you can control, because when you do that you no longer brace for a catastrophe, but prepare to respond to a challenge*, and regardless of the answer, a challenge always teaches you something!

That is what suffering is! That is why the behaviour we have will never regard suffering as a challenge, as something to learn from, but as a catastrophe, and that is why we must change it through nobility! A challenge either teaches you what to do next time, or it teaches you that you managed to learn from last time, but that only happens when you regard it as a challenge!

Just like the first stage of competence, you must transform your life voluntarily, you must look at the 'chaos' you define as suffering, realise that it is a result of your choices, realise that you can change your choices, realise that your new behaviour can become a habit after engaging for 22-to-28 days in it, and consequently transform your suffering in habitual order!

Speaking of learning from challenges and habits, the fastest way to not repeat history is by learning about it, and one part of history that helped me relieve suffering is the history of Stoicism, and it is usually divided in two: Greek & Roman Stoics. Thus, I say now, we must look at the bright minds of the past and of the present, and understand what they have to say. Though they are not with us anymore, their purpose to better this world and future generations to come is still present through their writings, so if the ability to change something is present, then so too is the soul and memory of a departed!

So learn from your forefathers! Learn from the greatest minds of the Greeks, learn from the greatest minds of the Romans! Let their suffering give you power, for you are not alone in your despair! Let their lessons give you power, for you too can rise like they did before! Let their minds open yours, like the minds of their forefathers opened theirs! Let you be to the greatest minds of Greek and Roman Stoics what Zeno of Citium was to Socrates, what Chrysippus was to Zeno, what Marcus Aurelius was to Rusticus! Let you be the greatest student to life!

Let you be noble!

FOREGONE

Chapter I

PRUDENCE

If you are pained by any external thing, it is not this thing that disturbs you, but your own judgment about it. And it is in your power to wipe out this judgment now.
— MARCUS AURELIUS

YOU ARE NOT PRUDENT

What is prudence? Prudence is reason. It is the trait that guides decision making. It is the trait that teaches us to judge correctly, to define, categorise, and know what's right and wrong in any situation given. It is the mother of all other cardinal virtues.

We cannot be evil & prudent at the same time, for prudence stems from the goodness of the heart. So if prudence defines what is good, then it is the measurement of justice, fortitude, and temper, for justice cannot be served without defining what is good and bad, fortitude cannot fight against unrecognisable evil, and temper can't exist if there's no delimitation to how much good is good, and how much bad is bad.

THE BEHAVIOUR OF PRUDENCE

What does it mean to be good? To be good means to discern between good and evil, to choose to be good through your actions, and to choose not to be evil unless in self-defence. To choose not to inflict misery, be it on yourself or another. What does it mean to not inflict misery? To not inflict misery means to not hurt physically or mentally. To not cause suffering. How does one get to not suffer physically or mentally? One starts by looking at their behaviour, at what specifically isn't good, and by taking the action to correct that.

We all have a basic definition of moral, of good, of righteous. Regardless if we are religious or not, the 6 commandments God has for humans is a good point to start if we don't know how to be good:

- **Honour your father and your mother**. It refers to gratitude. Remember to be grateful for your parents. Remember to be grateful for your health, and for being able to get up and make your life better by even 1% than last week, instead of complaining. Realise how depressed you'd be if your health left you and you were sick and yearning for another day. How miserable you'd be if the phone you're angry at broke, if the house you live in and hate would break down and now you'd be on the streets, if the little amount of privilege you have now would be taken away.
- **You shall not murder**. It refers to understanding your darkness. Know that you cannot control your emotions, but you can understand them. Because you have control over your mind, and by extension your choices, know that you can control your actions, so don't let your emotions control your actions, let your actions control your emotions!
- **You shall not commit adultery**. It refers to being assertive. You must not indulge in pleasure at the expense of another's happiness. You must not put another's entire disposition in peril for you to have pleasure!
- **You shall not steal**. It refers to not assuming. You must remember that perception is the sum of information processed by our senses (what we feel, see, and hear). Thus, although our perceptions reflect our life, it does not reflect reality. We must then allow ourselves to question and pursue deeper understanding, and not steal another's right to explain themselves. Things are not what they seem, and we should see them for what they are, not how we want them to be!
- **You shall not bear false witness against your neighbour**. It refers to lying. Know that lying is detrimental to both ourselves, and the others. There is only temporary benefit to be gained from it, and potentially permanent detriments to be gained.
- **You shall not covet**. It refers to respect. In life we must not denigrate those who made it, but applaud them. We must respect

their hard work, not bring them down because we wish to avoid the hard work we didn't put in!

WHY YOU AREN'T PRUDENT

As life showed us, breaking the law has consequences. The bigger the felony, the bigger the consequences. Thus, we must question our behaviour when we look at the day before:

- Did we blame someone for our mistake?
- Did we raise our voice?
- Did we send any spiteful messages?
- Did we assume? Did we show aggressiveness or passiveness?
- Did we lie to ourselves or others?
- Did we respect ourselves and the others?
- Did we concern ourselves with things we have no control over?
- Did we work on bettering our future through our actions?

The answer is usually yes and no. Where we might be proud about some answers, we aren't about others. Remember that to fall is not bad, to refuse to get up is. In the same way, to make a mistake is not bad, but to refuse to learn from it is. Therefore, the reason why you aren't prudent is because you didn't learn from all the instances life gave you, from all the tests that you came against. Would a good person yell? Assume? Disrespect another? Waste a day? I think not.

HOW TO BE PRUDENT

To be prudent is to define what it means to be good, and what it means to be bad. It is the compartmentalisation of good and bad within defined parameters. It also means to act good, not only know good.

This applies to absolutely every situation we're in. Whatever we do, we must ask ourselves: 'what is the right solution in this situation?'. It is such a sensitive subject that it can be anything that we will talk about in section 2:

- It's the conscious choice to understand what is good and bad, first of all. If we do not know, we can use the 6 commandments God has for humans as a starting point.
- It's the choice to focus on what we can control, and look at our life and everything around us that needs fixing, as opposed to blaming everything on the person next to us, or on an 'outside force' that has something against us and keeps us in this suffering loop.
- It's the choice to question our behaviour and separate our actions in 'noble' and 'not noble'. To realise that we are susceptible to losing control to our feelings, and that it isn't just to behave this way!
- It's the choice to accept our darkness, instead of allowing it to control us. That which we avoid is that which controls us, for fear is the avoidance of dealing with a situation, and fear is driving us away from confronting a situation over which we believe to have no control.
- It's the choice to listen to another and get the full picture, instead of giving in to our impulses to cut mid-way and give our impression. A final detail can reverse the situation 100%, so listen. + & -
- It's the choice to be assertive, to stand up for our right to happiness, but to also respect another's happiness, as opposed to being aggressive and taking their rights, or passive and surrendering ours.

In section 2 we will discuss the 'rules' that will give us a better understanding of the four cardinal virtues, and everything will make more sense then. For now, focus on understanding that the first step away from suffering and towards peace is to focus on what you can control: your choice to separate good from evil, and your choice to act good from now on.

The dagger of sentiment can only hurt your feelings if you stab yourself with it, for only you can put sentiment behind another's words.

Chapter II

JUSTICE

In the end, what would you gain from everlasting remembrance? Absolutely nothing. So what is left worth living for? This alone: justice in thought, goodness in action, speech that cannot deceive, and a disposition glad of whatever comes, welcoming it as necessary, as familiar, as flowing from the same source and fountain as yourself.
— MARCUS AURELIUS

YOU ARE NOT JUST

What is justice? Justice is the behaviour of prudence shown through our actions. It is the gratitude we have to God for what we are, and the respect we show others by treating them equal, honest, fair. It is prudence manifested through behaviour.

Justice is concerned with our will, with our reason, and cannot be manifested if good and evil is not defined. The way you research what foods a baby can eat is the same way you research what is good and what is bad. You can't just go ahead and feed the baby whatever, and the same applies when it comes to your behaviour: you can't just go ahead and behave however your impulses lead you to behave. Just as babies get sick from food, so too can people get sick of your behaviour. So you must research what you do before you do anything. Also, in contrast to babies, people can punch.

THE BEHAVIOUR OF JUSTICE

What does it mean to be just? To be just means to show respect to others. It stems from showing respect to yourself first, and consequently by showing respect to others. If you can't respect yourself then you can't respect others:

- How can you respect another if you do not know what is good and evil?
- How can you respect another if you do not understand your behaviour?
- How can you respect another if you do not listen to understand them?
- How can you respect another if you do not pay your dues to them?
- How can you respect another if you judge them on their genetic features?
- How can you respect another if you do not respect their choices?
- How can you respect another if you get mad at them?

What I mean by respecting yourself is that you don't know how to be good to others if you aren't good to yourself, and that starts by understanding what is good and what is evil. Realise that just as we have rights, so do the others, and since we are all equal, that we are not above them. What if the roles were reversed and nobody would listen to you, if everyone would get mad at you, if everyone would forget the help you gave and refused to help you, if everyone judged you on your gender, or race, or the shape of your nose, if everyone was rude to you? That wouldn't be so good, would it? Then don't do it to others!

Respect is a very broad topic, as you can see, but worry not. As mentioned before, section 1 is the appetizer, and the main course which breaks down the content of this section in smaller lessons is section 2.

WHY YOU AREN'T JUST

If justice is the manifestation of prudence through our actions, and prudence is the measurement of justice, then we aren't just because our actions don't represent that which we supposedly think: to be good. Because we aren't good to ourselves. How can we respect others if we can't respect ourselves? How can we respect ourselves if we don't know what is good? How can we give others their due when we don't know what those are? How can we respect them when our bad actions restrict the exercise of their rights?

To top that:

- If you do not define good and evil for yourself, why do you expect others to define it for themselves? Be good!
- If you do not question your behaviour, why do you expect others to question theirs? Be scrutinising!
- If you don't act good to others, why do you expect others to be good to you? Be righteous!
- If you don't listen to what others say, why do you expect others to listen to what you have to say? Be gentle!
- If you don't pay your dues to others, why do you expect others to help you? Be honourable!
- If you judge someone based on their race, gender, or emotions, instead of their actions (that which they can control), how do you expect people to accept you, to support you? Focus on what you can control!
- If you do not respect others' choices, how do you expect people to respect yours? Be reasonable!
- If you do not stand by your choices, how do you expect people to take you seriously? Be assertive!
- If you get mad at others' behaviours as a lack of understanding yourself, how do you expect others to not get mad at your behaviour as a lack of understanding themselves? Be realistic!

HOW TO BE JUST

On paper it seems easy, and that is to make sure to give everyone their due: punishment and rewards, honour and shame, courage and fear, taxes and rebates.

Injustice is the avoidance of correct action, and decision to act based on temporary emotions. It is the refusal to respect the others' rights. Briefly put, when you act based on your emotions and not on hard-facts, on evidence, on reality, or better said, on prudence, you are usually committing an injustice.

As a consequence we don't treat everyone equally, and to prove that we can look at yesterday's actions and ask ourselves:

- Did we give everyone their due, regardless of what we think of them?
- Did we shame someone? Ethnically? Genderly?
- Did we denigrate someone?
- Did we ask for more than something is worth?

Thus, we must remember the 6 commandments God gave humans:

- **Honour your father and your mother**. Be just and grateful!
- **You shall not murder**. Be just and respect others' rights to life!
- **You shall not commit adultery**. Be just and respect others' rights to happiness!
- **You shall not steal**. Be just and respect others' hard work!
- **You shall not bear false witness against your neighbour**. Be just and respect the truth!
- **You shall not covet**. Be just and respect their possessions!

This is what it means to be just:

To understand and respect the rights of others by understanding what their rights are, and that is by learning to be respectful to yourself first.

Chapter III
FORTITUDE

Circumstances don't make the man, they only reveal him to himself.
— EPICTETUS

YOU ARE NOT BRAVE

What is fortitude? Fortitude is the strength to be committed to your reason, to do what you proposed to do, be that to be good in general, or to stick to a plan. Fortitude is not the lack of fear but the acceptance of it, and the subsequent transformation of fear in a challenge, not a detriment. It is the ability to keep your ship steady in the storm, and the realisation that you must get the ship to the other side, that you must do what's right, regardless of the storm. And when you are in the storm remember that you can gain benefits from it, it can make you a better sailor if you pay attention, so learn what you can and keep moving forward! Reach the destination you set, regardless of the fear!

Fortitude is always exercised with reason, for you cannot be strong if you do not know what you are strong for. The easiest thing that comes to my mind is people who go on a diet (I don't refer to online diets, I'm talking about a professionally-custom-tailored diet from a nutritionist). Even the guided ones can lose their balance on the path and step outside the road. Certain factors like taste and low energy can feel daunting, but the strong ones find the resolution to push through. They're the ones who understood before they started that they're going to have lower energy than normal on this diet, the ones who realise that they're not in for taste the diet has. They're the ones who will push through because they motivate themselves by thinking about the benefits to be gained from this diet, and understand that if it was easy everyone would have done it. Delayed gratification.

THE BEHAVIOUR OF FORTITUDE

Fortitude is exercised with reason, and it assesses the true nature and value of our purpose. It gives us power to not stray from the road, and it keeps our eyes on the prize. It assesses whether something is worth fighting for, it strengthens our resolve if that is the case, it helps us resist temptation and overcome weakness, and it makes us appreciate the sacrifice we make for the greater good.

If prudence decides that what is good for us is a diet, and justice decides that abstaining from fast-food and sweets is the right thing to do, then we rely on fortitude to sustain that behaviour through thick and thin. *Fortitude is the strength within that enables us to stay on the path, and it stems from understanding our motivation to do what we plan on doing* (more in section 3, chapter 4: *The principle of the question 'why?'*).

WHY YOU AREN'T BRAVE

There are a million reasons to not be brave, but only one reason to be brave: *you only live once, and the pain of discipline is infinitely smaller than the pain of regret.* I do not plan on being nihilistic, depressed, morbid and whatnot, but unfortunately we all die someday. We have no control over that, but we have control over our life and over our choices, and although we cannot control death, we can choose how we live.

But before we live a good life we must first want a good life! Why would we want a good life? So that we may have peace, and potentially happiness, and surely to not suffer! What is a good life made of if not of good choices, those which are different from the ones we currently take? Thus we must make a change, even if changes are scary.

Changes are something new, and although we suffer now, we are comfortable in our suffering, and we don't want more suffering on top of that. We don't want our friends to laugh at us for doing something new, we don't want to lose our 'friends' for changing ourselves and refusing to engage in behaviour we no longer consider good, we don't want to lose the illusion of happiness food brings us and change our diet, we don't want to lose the illusion of happiness from staying up late with friends and change ourselves, we don't want to invest the little time we have every day towards discovering ourself and our potential with the purpose of changing our life into something we might like. We're tired, and we don't want to change. It's scary. There's so many variables that can occur, there are so many things to learn, so many things to change. 'I can't do that!'.

HOW TO BE BRAVE

YES YOU CAN! Remember that when the going gets tough, the tough get going! Just as it took the choices of the past five years to be who you are today, so too will it take you the next five years to change yourself in the person you want to be.

'That's making things worse! How is this helping?', you ask. You're focusing on the wrong thing! It's not that it's going to take a lot of time to change, it's that you have a lot of time to change! It's not that you will change in five years, it's that you will change one day at a time for the better, for five years! Or less than five years! You think where you are is better? It's not. Even if you're the king of the mountain you can still find ways to be better. There is always a way to be better, regardless if you are a wreck or a pearl! We all start somewhere, but we have to start, and that is by making a plan and following it with the focus in mind that we will emerge victorious! By being brave!

'Okay, so how do I become brave?', you ask. *You find the answer to the question 'why?'*. Whenever we plan on doing something, for example to start being prudent, we must remember that we will be tested (thanks to the four stages of competence). So when we get in a situation where we are about to lose control, where we are about to assume, to get angry, to yell or to smash, we must remember the answer we set behind the question 'why do I want to be prudent?', which is 'to suffer less'. And that answer will give us strength because fortitude is exercised with reason, and if we truly wish to suffer less, then we will truly focus on doing our best to calm down in heated moments. We will be prudent. We will be brave. We will pass the storm even if it takes us five years!

Chapter IIII

TEMPERANCE

There is no difference between knowledge and temperance; for he who knows what is good and embraces it, who knows what is bad and avoids it, is learned and temperate.
— SOCRATES

YOU ARE NOT TEMPERED

What is temperance? Temperance is wisdom. It is the wisdom to know what is good and what is bad, and even more, to know how much good is good, and how much bad is bad, for good can become bad.

It is the ability to regulate appetite and moderate emotions. A portion of food is health, three portions of food is diabetes. Capisce?

THE BEHAVIOUR OF TEMPERANCE

Before we discuss about the SoS and SoH, let us take some examples of wrong judgements. Everything (anger, assuming, passiveness, love, respect, modesty, etc.) is a result of our minds, devoid of external forces.

Just as you continue on your way to work without being hurt by the fact that someone somewhere is (unbeknownst to you) talking bad about you, so too can you continue to work without being hurt if those people said something bad about you in front of you. Why? Because it isn't the words that count, but the actions.

Let's explain:

- **ANGER** – Anger comes from inside of you, and it can be triggered by multiple factors: what someone said, what someone did, what you said, what you did. ***Briefly, it stems from not focusing on what you can control: that you can rectify a situation, or not (and in either case, why bother?).*** You can be mad because, after going to a coffee shop for so long and warming up to everyone, the lady from the coffee shop laughed at you when you told her your plan to write a book (me). Nobody likes to be hurt, especially by people we have close to our hearts, like friends and family. But you must be tempered and understand that she has the right to have an opinion, and although she decided to laugh, we can still control the situation: we can choose to realise that we made a mistake and believed her to be different (because of our perception), we can choose to not speak to her about our future anymore. We can realise that the passion we have hasn't dimmed because she laughed at us, for we will still eat, drink, work, and sleep the same. Do the words of people from middle-school affect the way I wake up today? I don't even remember their words!

- **ASSUMING** – Assuming comes from inside of you, and it can be triggered by multiple factors: what you heard, what you saw, what you felt, what someone told you, etc. ***Basically, it stems from not focusing on what you can control: that you can always research a topic and see what the reality is, instead of taking for granted your perception. Also, you cannot control events, so don't take things for granted.*** You can assume that someone forgot about your birthday and be sad all day, only to find a surprise birthday party home. You can assume that the answers you gave in a test were correct and submit, only to find later that you should've double checked in order to spot your errors and get a better grade. You can assume that you will get a promotion, and realise that you made a mistake by taking things for granted.

- **EVERY OTHER NEGATIVE EMOTION** – Basically everything is made up by our judgement, regulated by our nervous system, and controlled by our ego. It's the same as not getting mad at our mates when they curse us (because we know that their words are actually of love), and getting mad at the words of a stranger (because we somehow give those words weight). We can only hurt if we choose to be hurt, so choose to have no opinion about their opinion. We will discuss this in section 2 and 3.

Now the SoS and SoH:

The SoS is the *Sense of Shame*, and its purpose is to bring attention to the feelings we get when we lose control, like overeating, getting mad, assuming things, and being proven wrong. It is the sense that brings disgrace, confusion, and embarrassment, and it stems from being intemperate in our actions.

The SoH is the *Sense of Honour*, and its purpose is to bring attention to the feelings we have when we maintain control, like acting according to a schedule, maintaining our composure in an argument, and doing the right thing, generally speaking. It is the sense that brings dignity, esteem, and love, and it stems from practicing temperance.

WHY YOU AREN'T TEMPERED

Let's look at the two examples I gave above: anger and assuming.

You cannot feel dignity when you assume something and get it wrong. You feel embarrassment. You cannot feel love when you yell at someone. You feel confusion. You cannot feel esteem when you get mad as a result of your choices. You feel disgrace.

You can feel dignity when you question someone or something and realise that what you thought about that someone or something was not what it actually was. You can feel love when you realise that you need to be the bigger person, when you realise that no amount of talking can help a person that doesn't want to be helped, a person who's thick skull is simply not ready for the conversation you have to offer. That is self-love. You can feel esteem when you temperate yourself and realise that you can suffer more in your imagination through the misery inflicted by an anger born of your assumptions than you'd 'suffer' if you picked up the phone and asked for clarification.

HOW TO BE TEMPERED

You get tempered by setting a limit on good, and a limit on bad. By defining how much good is good, and how much bad is bad. Whatever that may be.

'But how do I know where to set the limit?', you ask. You make a plan that focuses on weekly/monthly incrementations. Just as you know that next month you have to do more push-ups in order to stimulate muscle growth, so too do you know that more than one burger will stimulate fat gain.

You have a potential, and everything in your day should revolve around bringing your potential to surface. As we will discuss in section 3, we will try to discover the addictions around us (Netflix, fast-food, excessive entourage, etc.), and make a plan that will focus our hours on nurturing that potential.

To give a sneak peek of section 3: say you wish to discover your talent. Using the steps in each chapter of section 3, you will go from understanding:

- The importance of a well-rested nervous system.
- The fact that you can't be *truly* happy without a purpose.
- The way to discover your talent by using *the creative process.*
- That a strong answer that justifies what you do is required to not be lazy.
- That we lie to ourselves, and that we must acknowledge the lies.
- That we must look at our addictions and remove them using a schedule.
- That we must have a plan for the future to keep us accountable.
- That we must compare only to past-selves, and with others for sport.

The same thing applies to everything, not only to talent:

Going on a diet? Define the result you want to achieve, find a strong answer behind your reason to achieve that goal, stop lying to yourself that you can eat pizza daily because you'll lose it with cardio, remove sweet foods from your house, make a plan to keep yourself accountable for the next two or three months while you diet, and most importantly: don't compare your results with another. *A burger per week isn't bad, five burgers are. Know the limit.*

FOREGONE

Want to be a better person? Let's say you start by focusing on the first rule of section 2, *Focus on what you can control.* You do that for one month continuously, and you pay attention to every situation you can. You define the result you want to achieve (to understand that you don't need to be angry on the things you can't control), you find a good motivation (suffer less), you stop lying to yourself (stop shifting blame from yourself to others), and have a little calendar in your house where you can mark every day where you managed to differentiate and categorise the things you can and can't control. Every time you resist getting mad at what you can't control you add a '*' symbol. Every time you get mad at what you can't control you add a '!' symbol. You increase your tolerance to it by making sure you keep a streak going on, and you know that beating your previous tolerance record is good, and going under your previous tolerance record is bad.

Everything starts with the four stages of competence, so it's up to you to realise the importance of being tempered. Good luck, I believe in you!

FOREGONE

Chapter V
THE ROOM

If you can't even clean up your own room, who are you to give advice to the world?
— JORDAN B. PETERSON

Mr. Jordan B. Peterson

Mr. Jordan B. Peterson is a Canadian clinical psychologist that has changed my life. Two years ago I was in a dark place, lost again, suffering, and I discovered him whilst searching for articles and videos about depression and serotonin.

He has a YouTube video where he talked about a room. He explained that our minds are alike this room, and that if our room is tidy then so too is our life, and if our room is messy then so too is our mind. The only thing he asks of us is to put our room in order. There are so many great videos from him you can watch that boredom is a choice.

WHAT IS THE ROOM?

The room is at first a literal place, and then a metaphorical one.

In the first instance, *the room* is literally our room. The box with four walls where we sleep. The place where we have our bed, our desk, and whatever else is in a room.

In the second instance, *the room* is our life. Our job. Our friends. Our activities. Our judgement. Our choices.

The subject of 'cleaning your room' has two purposes (that I can see so far), with the first being to tidy up you room, and the second being to tidy up your life.

WHY TIDY UP YOUR ROOM?

After researching Stoicism (see section 2, most of the rules are derived from it and will help you clean up your room), I saw certain rules apply when I was 'cleaning my room'.

This is only my interpretation: since actions lead to questions, and questions lead to development, instead of trying to explain to you the mechanism behind everything, Mr. Peterson just gave you a task. A task which, if you pursue, will lead to you feeling better. As a result of feeling better, you will start to ask questions. With questions comes understanding, and with wisdom comes peace. So instead of telling you to better your life through 100 steps and to try to convince you that those steps are necessary, he gave you a task which you can pursue, if you wish, and get to be better as a result, both in mind and spirit.

Earlier I said that I can see two purposes to cleaning your room. The first phase is to actually tidy up your room, the box you live in. What is the purpose of that? Behind this activity there is a cascade of thoughts that occur, and this activity works like this:

- First you *must* declare what is order and what is chaos, and you must categorise it in good and evil, otherwise you don't know how to tidy it up (prudence).
- Second, you *must* acknowledge that your room is not in order, for you cannot clean something if you do not acknowledge it as dirty (justice).
- Third, you *must* declare that you have to start someday, because if you don't pick up your clothes and wash them, one day you won't have anything to wear (fortitude).
- Lastly, you *must* start keeping your room clean, and do that every day. Cleaning is not done, but maintained (temperance).

The second phase is to apply the same principle, but to your life. To look at your life like you look at your room, and to start tidying up.

What is the purpose? To apply the cascade of virtues and to remove your suffering, and it works like this:

- First, you *must* declare what is good and what is evil, and you must categorise your behaviour in 'actions that are noble' and 'actions that are not noble'. You can't perform 'actions that are noble' if you don't know the difference between good and evil (prudence).
- Second, you *must* acknowledge that you engage in 'actions that aren't noble', for you can't change if you do not realise that a change is needed (justice).
- Third, you *must* declare that you have to start someday, because you cannot just let suffering dictate your life. You have only one life, and you have the power to make a change (fortitude).
- Lastly, you must maintain this life by engaging in 'actions that are noble', for you shouldn't be a part of the never ending cycle where you have peace today and sorrow tomorrow (temperance). Why? Because you have the power inside of you to be better, and you have the right to not suffer!

Interesting how there are four steps, just like the four stages of competence mentioned in *Chapter Nulla*. Maybe there is a correlation between them?

WHAT IS IN YOUR ROOM?

In your room there are problems to be addressed, and issues to be fixed. Every dirty cup, plate, socks, and everything else that has been put there by you can also be removed by you. Why? Because you are not chained! You have control! As we will see in section 2, chapter 1A: *Focus on what you can control,* you have control over your mind. This is the greatest gift life gave us, and if we lack wisdom it can be our biggest curse.

The reason I say curse is because we aren't aware of the fact that we have control over our mind, and by extension our choices, and that a choice repeated daily leads to 'perfection'. That'd be a great thing to teach in school.

On top of that, everything is a concept of the mind. Your perception, your expectations, your anger, your fear, your tendency to assume. Everything is up there, not outside of it. So if someone angers you, it angers you because you let yourself angered, and you think them to be the problem, when the problem is your judgement about the anger itself. The problem is not the problem, the problem is the attitude about the problem.

So to answer this subsection, in our room are the multitude of choices we took that brought us to the suffering we are currently experiencing, whatever form that is. Our room is our suffering, and cleaning it is fortifying ourselves with wisdom in order to remove suffering.

Suffering can be anything: your job, your colleagues, your weight, your lack of purpose, your fear. And you know what? All of those can be changed, because all of those are within your control: you can always search for a new job. You can always learn to expect less from your colleagues. You can always lose weight. You can always search and discover your purpose. You can always conquer the fear to do all of those things, *but you must first choose!* You must choose to change! You must choose to clean up your room! You must choose to remove suffering from your life!

HOW TO TIDY UP YOUR ROOM?

First of all, you break your suffering in proximity circles, and you separate your circles by intensity levels:

- *L1* - First level is the easy intensity. It is composed of things that need minimum time and effort to change (be it five minutes or one day). For example: your posture, your hydration, your decision to clean your room (yes, even in the second phase where you clean your metaphorical room you must still clean your actual room. Nobody gets away from the daily dust!). This is the equivalent of the first two stages of competence.
- *L2* - Second level is the medium intensity. It is composed of things that need medium time and effort to change (be it one month or six). For example: a diet, researching and understanding a subject, making sure to respect the rules you set out respect, etc. This is the equivalent of stage three of competence.

- *L3* - Third level is the hard intensity. It is composed of things that need years, like being noble and realising that you should focus only on what you can control, on questioning your behaviour, on accepting your darkness, on not assuming, on being assertive, on listening to understand, on realising your worth, on being grateful, etc. This is the equivalent of the last stage of competence.

Second of all, you look at your life and you start addressing everything you are suffering about, and you add them an intensity level number. So if you have a banana-shape-posture, that's *L1*, if you're on a diet that's *L2* (suffering isn't quitting your diet, it's adjusting it if it's wrong and pushing through with bravery), and if you want to find peace and happiness that's *L2/L3*, depending on where you are with your understanding of life. *Briefly put, you ask yourself 'what am I angry about nowadays?', and you write it on a paper so you don't forget.*

I'm going to give some examples from my life, and I hope that this will be a good model to understand how to structure your problems according to the intensity levels:

My main problem in life was anger. I grew up in an angry country where Dunning-Krueger-elitists exist. Every one of them believes itself to be a 'genius', and yet their actions show otherwise. That's how you discover great people: those who talk a little about their life and are always seen doing something. Those who lead by example and allow their actions to show their philosophy, as opposed to those who have graduated the school of criticism and talk about their imaginary achievements. That's why a lot of people speak and yet have nothing to say: because it's easier to gain honour through words (lying) than it is to gain through sweat and hard work.

Besides that, I always had weight problems, consistency problems, basically the full 'dropped in the middle of the dessert without a map' problems. I'm going to spare you the details and tell you this: although I am grateful for my mates for always supporting me, the only help that healed my soul was philosophy and wisdom. Only through wisdom did I realise that I have no reason to complain about anything in life, and that just as I'm hungry and can get up to cook, so too can I feel pain and start taking the actions to remove it.

Through the wisdom gained from Stoicism, philosophy, and Mr. Peterson, I have removed a lot of suffering from my life, invited peace, and even brought along happiness. *But first I had to choose to change my life! To focus on what I can control, and that is my choice to be better!* First I had to realise that only through change can I not suffer anymore (first stage of competence).

Through the realisation of the power I have over my choices, I have started pursuing wisdom in order to address certain issues:

- Tired of always being angry? I searched for articles on Google, as simply as opening a computer, going to Google and typing 'what is anger?' (I chose to do something about it instead of complaining about it). *L3*
- Not knowing how to do proper gymnastics, and didn't have the money for a personal trainer? Saved enough money to purchase a personal trainer course (chose to save money). *L2*
- Tired of always losing weight and then gaining it back, never truly understanding what to believe and what not from all these crash (more like crush) diets from the internet? Saved enough money to purchase a nutritionist course (chose to save money). *L2*
- Everything I did was according to the question 'so can I do something about it?', and if the answer was yes, then I continued with 'so why am I complaining?'. If the answer was no, then I continued with 'so why am I complaining?'. The only point of complaining is to bring to attention the need for change. That's all there is to it, because if there wasn't pain then there wouldn't be a need for change, but a lot of people get stuck here and give up (second stage of competence).

Third of all, you do not give up, you do not forget where you came from, you do not forget that if you give up and go back where you came from initially it wouldn't be good, because when you were there you wished to be where you are now. You keep on pushing, on learning, on applying, even if the world will be against you (as long as what you're doing is morally right and you're not overdoing it).

There's no reason to go back, but there is a reason to look back: to learn to be grateful for what you have, and to strengthen your bravery in those days where you tremble, for if you fall and don't get up you go back where you came from. So look at your present-self and realise the amazing strength you display by having pushed so far, and feel your bravery rejuvenate as a result of that. Only a little further now (third stage of competence)!

Although not there yet, I am working towards my fourth step. That step where nobility will be my second nature. That step where, for example, I won't even think about not assuming (like I am right now), but instinctively know that I must not assume. That step where everything balances, where there is equilibrium. That step where I master that which I preach. That step where my philosophy is easily read through my actions.

This is what I'm trying to do with this book: help, but not invade. Help, but not control. I want to realise that I have the right to happiness, and it does not depend on another, for all feelings and thoughts springs from within me. I can be happy without depending on another, I can be peaceful without depending on another, and although it seems like I am discarding the other, know that I am not. For I cannot be happy without helping another.

I recently came across a quote from Seneca, one of the three great Roman stoics, and he puts it better than I do: 'In this sense the wise man is self-sufficient, that he can do without friends, not that he desires to do without them. When I say 'can,' I mean this: he endures the loss of a friend with equanimity.'. Be strong alone, but wish not to be alone.

Life is a beautiful balance between being good and helping others.

FOREGONE

WHO ARE YOU?

FOREGONE

Chapter Ω

KNOW WHO YOU ARE

Don't accept your dog's admiration as conclusive evidence that you are wonderful.
— ANN LANDERS

WHO ARE YOU?

If you ask yourself right now *'who am I?'*, what would your answer be? Would you state your name? Your profession? Your status in society? Your likes and dislikes? What would you say?

The reason I'm asking this is because lately I've been dealing with this question on a personal level, and I think I understand why it is asked. This isn't a question that needs to have an answer, not an immediate one anyway, instead it's a question made to drive you towards a creative process that ultimately leads to *discovering your ego & dissolving it thereafter.*

EGO. Why is this short word so important, why does everything revolve around it, what value lies in discovering its meaning, and should you venture towards discovering it? YES. YOU. SHOULD, so let's start by understanding its etymology first. Ego is present in both Latin and Greek, and it is the word that means 'I', the self, the id of a person. However, in our context we will use the English meaning of the word.

What does ego mean in English? Ego means *your sense of self-importance*, the sense that encapsulates your entire being up to this point. We know that someone with a big ego is someone who arrogantly thinks about itself as number one, but generally speaking, ego is nothing more than a library of information manifested through fanatic faith in oneself.

'A library of information manifested through fanatic faith in oneself?', you ask. Yes, an ego is a library of trial-and-error activities. It is the sum of the reasons you have for everything you experienced and did in your life. The ego hoards the knowledge of your behaviour, be it your preferences or your reaction to stimuli. Ergo, **EGO is information.**

What purpose does the ego serve? Ego is necessary to assemble your character traits, your wishes, your likes and dislikes, your life goal, and your motivation. Aswell as the sense of self-importance, the ego is also your friend for a while because it is your sense of egoism, that particular sense of doing things for yourself that protects you from social expectations. In my opinion, ego is for the character what the deciduous teeth are for the baby: the first step of experimenting growth. Fortunately nothing stays the same, and as we lose our deciduous teeth and gain the real teeth thereafter, so too must we lose our ego in order to find ourselves. Our *true* selves, *who we want to be.*

Surprisingly, some people get stuck with their ego their entire life. The ego is strong, and it has been with you since you were old enough to understand reality. Its influence is very strong and, without an open mind for open ended questions, you will not reach your true self anytime soon. The reason for that is because nobody likes to change, so dissolving it won't be a walk in the park either (if you even get to think about dissolving it). 'But why is it important to dissolve the ego?', you ask. To answer your question simply, it's because *when your ego is present you do not know who you truly are.*

It is very important to stress that *who you think you are* is not *who you want to be/who you truly are*, because who you think you are in this exact moment is possibly dictated by your ego. If true, then you are who your ego dictates you are because you're sitting in the passenger seat of your body, with the ego at the wheel. This can be demonstrated through a simple example that only requires you to ask *'but why?'* a short number of times. Starting now, I will offer you an insight about how little you know yourself, and how big of an impact you can have on your peace by understanding yourself, so answer these questions one by one, and ask *'but why?'* thereafter:

- Why do I get mad when I do?
- Why do I assume when I do?
- Why do I focus on that which I can't control?
- Why don't I question my behaviour if it isn't noble?
- Why don't I try to be assertive?
- Why do I explain myself to others when I do?
- Why do I consider my worth is based on others' thoughts about me?
- Why do I compare myself with others when I do?
- Why do I lie to myself when I do?
- Why do I waste time with addictions when I do?
- Why do I fall in an illusion of progress when I work on something?

All of the above questions offer an insight into your behaviour, offer an insight into your suffering. How many times did we assume that something bad will happen, and had anxiety all day? How many times did we say 'yes' to someone when we should've said 'no', and regretted after? How many times did we lie to ourselves that we'll start Monday, and Monday never came? How many times did we avoid doing what we had to do because we're addicted to Netflix, or YouTube, or other form of media? What about when we waste time although we're right in front of our task, but the pencil needs sharpening and the laptop needs cleaning? Ever got mad when the weather ruined your perfect day, or when you got into an argument with someone and couldn't contain your emotions, and consequently your actions? Lastly, do you remember how you felt worthless because someone believed you're a waste of space, although they never appreciated your hard work? Yeah, me too.

You see, behaviour is teachable, and alike every lesson that you received from your parents and friends that you integrated in your behaviour, so too must you now integrate new behaviour by asking yourself questions. I wish to bring to life the behaviour of *questioning your feelings, thoughts, and actions,* and to implant it in your active conscience. Things in your life will change for the better once you'll start *objectively* analysing your behaviour and questioning your actions. Reading a book is hallucinating at a dead tree for a couple of hours, so in order to avoid that (and to make sure something sticks), we must also engage you, the reader, with small exercises. Exercises that will allow the book to pass through the lens of your logic in order to engage your ability to fathom the lesson at a personal level by comparing it to your personal experiences. These exercises will be present in every chapter under the form of questions.

So now you ask: 'well, I'm intrigued. What can we do about this ego? How do we find out who we are, and more importantly, *who we want to be?*'.

The process is very simple on paper: you question everything you do three to five times until you realise that you do not know why you're doing what you're doing. When you get to understand that your behaviour is set, but not in stone, and that you can question it and understand that you have no idea why you act the way you act, true growth occurs. With true growth life gets better, and the suffering lessens.

Life is suffering, and it will continue to be until we rectify our behaviour. It will continue to be until we:

- Realise that if we can't control a situation then we shouldn't bother.
- Stop having prejudice (it imprisons us, wastes time, and instils anxiety).
- Realise that understanding our emotions leads to controlling our actions.
- Learn that without saying 'no' we cannot negotiate and find our worth.
- Admit that others' opinions of us is not who we truly are.
- Realise that people don't know what we've been through, so we shouldn't compare with them since we don't know what they've been through.
- Stop explaining ourselves because we do not owe anything to anyone.
- Accept what lying to ourselves is doing to us and to our potential.
- Schedule short, medium, and long-term goals to eliminate addiction.
- Stop focusing on instant gratification.

This is what knowing yourself is about. It's about letting go of what you can't control. It's about scrutinizing your behaviour using the *'but why?'* system a sufficient number of times, usually three to five times until you get to the point where you realise that you truly don't know why you're doing what you're doing. You never truly understood why you act the way you act. It's about understanding your dark side and then accepting it in order to be calm and collected. It's about listening to understand the other, instead of listening to answer. Finally, it's about not taking critique from someone you wouldn't take advice from, even if that someone is your begotten persona!

What to take away: Most people are not who they think they are, and that is because of their ego. They are walking libraries of data who have been disconnected from the world and can't update. They only know one thing: that the other is always wrong.

FOREGONE

Chapter 1A

FOCUS ON WHAT YOU CAN CONTROL

Incredible change happens in your life when you decide to take control of what you do have power over instead of craving control over what you don't.
— STEVE MARABOLI

PURPOSE

The purpose of this chapter is to highlight how focusing on the things we can't control only wastes our time and increases our angst. You can't control the weather and stop the rain, but you can choose to take an umbrella! Note that this is the 1st part, 1A, of a two-part chapter.

INTROSPECTIVE

Stoicism is the philosophy that teaches not only self-control, but also how our destructive emotions arise from our poor judgement, and how to improve our judgement in order to *behave well and live well*. It is my honour and pleasure to open the book with my favourite topic, one that was discussed the most by the old masters: *control*. This chapter is the easiest to understand, and the hardest to master. From it everything starts and ends.

We must distinguish between the things that we should focus on, those we can control with our choices (like checking the weather news before going out), and the things that we shouldn't focus on, those that we can't control with our choices (like the fact that mother nature decided that today will rain).

Having said that, let's look at some thoughts we might have:

Why should I not focus on the things I can't control? If I manage to understand that some things are outside of my control, what will that realisation produce? What are the virtues that I will gain from understanding the things I can control? What is my mission?

DEFINE

What is *control*? *Control* is the ability to manipulate matter, be it animate or inanimate. The ability to manipulate inanimate matter, like a glass of water, results from your *will* and your *control* over your muscles, nerves, and every fine mechanism that allows the movement to be performed. But the mind is capable of even finer mechanisms, and since *control* comes in many shapes, people can use it to also manipulate animate matter, such as other people. Just pointing that out.

'So what do we actually have control over?', you ask. **We only have control over our mind, and by extension, our choices!** Let's define further:

- We do not have control over our bodies and organs, for we can eat all the antioxidants in the world and be hit by misfortune, while others smoke two packs a day and never get lung cancer.
- We do not have control over our genetics, for no matter how much we wish to be taller or prettier, it will not come to pass (yes, you can get plastic surgery, but that's not altering your genetics, is it?).
- We do not have control over people's behaviour. We can't make them stand on one foot by command. Not our parents, siblings, friends, nor strangers (different from manipulation, which is making someone believe that they want to do that 'something' that you want them to do).
- We do not have control over reality, but only over our understanding of it [can't make gravity stop... gravity-ing(?)].
- We do not have control over our emotions, but only over our choice to understand them.
- We do not have control over the past, for we can't change it, and not over future events outside of our control (so don't take things for granted, present or future). Here is where expectations are born, where our judgment gets clouded, where our heart starts hurting.

ILLUSTRATE

There are so many experiences I can summon to illustrate what focusing on the things you can't control looks like that, for the sake of our sanity, I will just list a couple of them. Please note that, although some might seem specific, *the mechanism behind this behaviour is the same for all situations in life: instead of focusing on what we can change, we focus on what we can't.*

About ourselves: How many times were we tired and complained about it? And day after day we repeated our behaviour, instead of changing it? *Why complain about being tired, instead of focusing on the things we can control*: categorising and removing from our schedule those tasks which are unimportant in order to gain time and improve our sleep. Don't meet every day with your mates to drink. Don't eat junk food before bedtime every day. Don't play video games and go to bed late. Don't have coffee after 15:00, etc.

About others: My mother and I were talking about the amount of likes she has on a post, about 40. She said that this is a record, and I contradicted her almost midsentence that her other posts have over 50 likes. She kept trying to tell me that that's not what she meant, but I kept contradicting her and telling her that I am on her page, looking at her other posts, and noticing that she has over 40 likes on all of them. You see, I had the correct information in front of me, so I couldn't be wrong, right? Wrong! Right as she was about to say that on posts with over 1000 or 2000 views she gets about 50 likes, whereas on this post that has only 230 views she got around 40 likes, I interrupted her three times. *I wasn't listening to understand, I was listening to answer. I was focusing on what I can't control: predicting what she wanted to say before she said it.* Fortunately, we bounced back easily, and the lesson was learned. Win-win!

About our surroundings: How many times have we yelled at our computer when the internet went out, especially when we were in the middle of doing something? *Why yell at a cable for five minutes instead of realising that we cannot control the situation, and that no amount of yelling will bring the internet back?* Instead, why not realise that the feeling of urgency to return to work instilled by the shock of being pulled out of deep concentration resulted from us focusing on that which we can't control: the inability to realise that the internet went out and that we can't control it, and that what is happening is exactly what is happening, nothing more and nothing less.

About the future (bonus): *How many times have we been hit by sadness when we took things for granted, or when we hoped for something, both of which stem from focusing on that which we can't control?* How many times have we questioned the world about its reason for being mean to us, about making us suffer, when in reality it was by our choices that the predicament we are in came to pass? Too many times we see things as we want them to be (it will work, it can't fail, I hope that won't happen, I hope I will win, I hope that it won't have consequences), and not as they truly are (whatever will happen, will happen. This is just a challenge for me, and this too shall pass. If it is born of my choices, then from my choices it will be solved).

There is nothing to be won from focusing on the things you can't control. Based on this, take a second to ask yourself: 'what is there to gain from focusing on the things I can't control?'. Answer truthfully to yourself before jumping to the next section.

REWARD

Overthinking. Anger. Anxiety. Sadness. Disappointment. That's the reward. Do you know what overthinking is?

Overthinking is the inability to categorise your thoughts in things that you should think a lot about, a little about, and none at all about. It's the inability to distinguish between the things you should focus on that you can control with your choices, and the things you shouldn't focus on since you can't control them with your choices.

Overthinking will happen when we focus on the things we can't control and don't ascertain whether we can do something about it or not: 'does X likes me; will I get that job; will the sun explode in my lifetime?'. Can you control those situations? Let's see:

- No, you cannot guess what is going up inside their head (but you can ask them what their feelings for you are).
- No, you cannot know if they have selected you out of all the X interviewees (but you can wait for a message and meanwhile change

your attention to what you have to do that day that you have control over).

- No, you cannot know if the sun will explode in your lifetime (and even if you did, you can't change that. You can only make peace with your life and focus on doing your best every day!)

ANALYSE

Based on this, let's agree to two things:

- *One:* you only have control over your mind, and by extension your choices. All you have to do in this life is look at a situation and ask yourself 'can I control this?', or 'so what other option is there that I can control?'.
- *Two:* let's take raining, for example. No matter how much you cry about it, the rain won't stop. If the rain won't stop regardless of your choices, then why bother? All you get is wasted time and effort. Raining isn't bad, because we can expect it by looking at the news, and we know it to be beneficial to life. The problem appears when we don't expect it. When we get taken by surprise, drenched and mad thereafter. That's the trick: realise that expected or unexpected, you can't control it, so why bother?

Epictetus says that it's not things that upset us, it's our judgment about them. Think about it. Most of the times the problem is not the problem, the problem is the attitude about the problem. It's so easy to complain about everything, it's so easy to blame 'the outside forces' for the predicament we're in, instead of accepting that most of the times it is our choices that led to our current situation. And if they didn't? Then we must realise that our judgement is to blame, which is still something we have control over. *Nobody is making you have expectations and perception, but yourself!* Read that again.

We can always look at something, accept that it happened, see what state it is in, ascertain whether we can fix it or not, question what choices we can take to make it better if we can fix it, get up, apply those choices, and then relax knowing that we will have at least one thing to be proud of when we go to bed today. Or we can scream at it for five minutes.

Note that there are cases when things happen that have no meaning. The world isn't perfect. Sometimes the internet drops. But we can choose to accept it, or to get mad at it.

UNDERSTAND

Control (and focusing on the things you can't control) comes in three general shapes:

- *About ourselves*: You can focus on the negatives in your life instead of doing something about it. But why? If your life is skipping on one leg, you have the ability to fix it (instead of complaining about it)!
- *About others*: You can focus on the negatives in someone's life instead of minding your own business. We've all assumed and said things to people that we shouldn't have said. But why? That's not noble, that's rude! Question your behaviour and rectify it!
- *About our surroundings*: You can focus on the negatives in life instead of realising that you can't control them. Starting from earthquakes, tsunamis, volcanoes, and ending with getting drenched by the rain, realising that you stepped in faeces, and noticing that your bus or train has been delayed. Regardless of how angry you get, the faeces are already on your shoes and the bus will be late. See things as they are, not as you want them to be.

Based on this, we must realise that we need to be open to the idea that what we're doing might be wrong in order to improve, and that blindly believing in something without research is the work of our ego, and thus immature. What better purpose can you have on this planet than to be better than you were yesterday (respectfully)?

OVERCOME

There is this old saying about a bird that sits on a branch that suddenly breaks, and the saying explains how the bird doesn't get scared because its trust is in its wings, not in the branch it sits on! Alike this saying, so too should we live our life: we should not focus on other people's opinions, thoughts, gossip, or other things they have (about us or not), nor should we focus on natural disasters, such as earthquakes, volcano eruptions, tsunamis. None are within our control.

We should instead focus on our choices, on our ability to fly from the branch that broke, on our ability to realise that whatever someone says, does, or thinks, does not impact our ability to spread our wings! Think about the internet and the rude people who curse you online for no reason. Do them saying those things make reality bend to their will, and all of a sudden you're stupid, and ugly, and useless? No! So why get mad about it?

You want the world to be better? Start by being a better person yourself. Focus on that which you can control, realise your mistakes, correct them. Be the person you want to see in the world, and then attract people who think like you! *Make nobility and virtue your philosophy, the thing you believe in, and let your actions represent that philosophy, not your words!*

Most of the times our ego whispers to us that we are right and that the other is wrong, or that life hates us and there must be a divine reason why something bad happened to us. ***Briefly, the ego will always search for ways to make us think that the problem is not ourselves, but some exterior force that we can't control,*** because if we would ever realise that we control our misfortune then that realisation would lead to change, and what do we know about the ego? That it doesn't want to change, so we must break this cycle! We must stop blaming others, and instead realise that we are to blame most of the times. The biggest lie our ego feeds us is that by another's choice we came to be in the predicament that we are in! Not by ours. It's time to change that!

'Great, so how do we focus on the things we can control? How do we break the cycle?', you ask.

First of all, **we remind ourselves that the only thing we have control over is our choices.** *Control* is the ability of our mind to interact with the external world. *Control* is, therefore, our active reaction to the world, and nothing more.

Second of all, **we question ourselves about the things we have control over.** We cannot control our genetics (taller, prettier, etc.), nor the parents we have been given, nor the hand we've been dealt to play, nor others' opinions, nor others' stimuli, nor a situation. We can only control our minds and our choices, and thus we can only control how we respond to a situation! Approach life like you would approach a test in school: check the questions, start answering, *and when you get stuck, move on to the next question!* You can't waste your precious time not getting a better score because you're stuck on something you don't understand. Move on! Focus on the questions you can answer, learn about those you can't answer, and do better next time!

Third of all, **we question whether our choices brought us in the state we're in.** You look objectively (as through the eyes of a stranger) at your past actions and at the predicament you're in, and ask yourself about who is to blame, regardless of the shape that predicament takes (your predicament is everything that is wrong with your 'room').

Lastly, **we question ourselves what choices we can take to improve the predicament we're in.** For me, it was to learn to question if I have control over a situation in order to stop being mad all the time.

Whatever we choose, we need to realise the importance of being present in the moment. You see, control (and by extension our choices) cannot be exercised on the past or on the future. The past cannot be changed, and the future hasn't arrived yet. The way your current-self is who you've formed yourself to be in the past five years is the same way your future-self will be in five years who you're forming yourself to be right now. You are the sum of your choices, and as you will see in the chapter *Addiction,* you can have a plan for the future, but the only way you can manifest it into reality is by controlling your daily choices. One choice at a time.

Having said this, let's look at this lesson's exercises:

Why should I not focus on the things I can't control? If I manage to understand that some things are outside of my control, what will that realisation produce? What are the virtues that I will gain from understanding the things I can control? What is my mission?

I'd like to ask you to answer these questions first by yourself, on a paper preferably in order to check what you know, what you've learned from this chapter, and what you don't know and can learn from the answers given from my perspective. Trust the process, and do this with every chapter's exercises.

I should not focus on the things I can't control because there is no reward for me there. However, a good reward is found in assessing whether something is in my control or not, and then acting on it. As you will see later in the section 3, chapter 2: *Happiness is the journey, not the destination,* we need to have an aim, a goal to pursue. Without it we can't usually have *true* happiness because of the balance between *the effort we make* and *the reward we get* that we will talk about later. How can you be happy at the end of the day if you didn't do anything productive? Based on that, remember that the 'rewards' you get from focusing on the things you can't control are: overthinking, anxiety, sadness, depression even.

Thus, If I manage to understand that some things are outside of my control, I will have more stability and tranquillity in my life:

- When I look at something that happened, like getting drenched by the rain for example, I need to question myself: 'can I do anything about it?'
- 'Not in this moment, no' is a good answer. So if I can't do anything about this, then I have no reason to get mad and to focus on it, right? That's right! But can I do anything about it tomorrow?
- 'Yes, I can check the news' is a good answer. I can't prevent the rain, but I can learn my lesson from yesterday's events, and focus on preventing this from happening again by focusing on my choices. The choice to check the news, the choice to grab my umbrella, *the choice to focus on what I can control*.

Now apply this with everything in life, from understanding that you can't help a person that doesn't want to be helped (a person who's thick skull is simply not ready for the conversation you have to offer), to not getting mad about anything outside of your control. You can be affected by it, but you can also get back up on your feet and realise that life is hard. I never said that life isn't hard. You will be tested. But life can be both hard and without suffering at the same time, as you will understand after reading this book twice.

The virtues that I will gain from understanding what I have control over are prudence, justice, fortitude, and temperance. Yes, this is a package deal, enjoy!

My mission is to confront every negative situation with the question 'is there anything I have control over in this situation?', and to focus on what I can control. Remember: you don't always need to have an opinion about an opinion.

What to take away: The only thing in your control is your mind and your choices. Not your body and its organs, not your genetics, not other people around you. Don't focus too much on the things outside of your control, there is no point. Instead, focus on making every day count, and on being better than yesterday! When you go to bed, what are you proud of?

Chapter 1B

QUESTION YOUR ACTIONS

Any person capable of angering you becomes your master;
he can anger you only when you permit yourself to be disturbed by him.
— EPICTETUS

PURPOSE

The purpose of this chapter attempts to highlight how blind we are when it comes to our behaviour, and how much we suffer because of it. Alike a car, if we do not perform an inspection we don't know if there's anything that requires change. This is the 2nd part, 1B, of chapter 1.

INTROSPECTIVE

When a washing machine breaks and we try to fix it, we usually begin by documenting ourselves about it in order to understand how it functions. If you don't know how it functions you don't know what's wrong with it, and you cannot repair that which you don't know is broken. Therefore, you must understand that in order to fix what is wrong with you, you need to allow yourself to acknowledge that which you might avoid acknowledging: that your actions are possibly flawed (prudence and justice). I can guarantee that you have no idea why you do some of the things that you do, and in order to find out if that's the case, you need to put your ego away. If my mission is successful, then this book will make you understand that most suffering in your life can be fixed with the correct choices, but first you have to know and understand yourself!

As mentioned in chapter *Know who you are*, it is important to add this behaviour of *questioning everything* to your character. I will dare and say that, as annoying as they are, kids who keep asking '*but why?*' are on the right track. It is this action of pursuing understanding that leads to the development of a healthy behaviour, in my opinion. Instead of accepting the ego's whispers that this is how things are, you can try and have a deeper understanding of *why* things are the way they are. Thus, we ask ourselves:

Why should I question everything? If I manage to stop seeing things at face-value what will that realisation produce? What are the virtues that I will gain from questioning everything? What is my mission?

DEFINE

What is *questioning*? *Questioning* is the active pursuit of deeper comprehension. It is the interest shown in something that attracts us manifested through query. It is the overrule of ego. It is the first step to reconnecting with peace. It is justice.

Questioning is the first step in realising that you have no idea who you really are. Look at the following questions:

- Why do I get mad when I do?
- Why do I assume when I do?
- Why do I focus on that which I can't control?
- Why don't I question my behaviour if it isn't noble?
- Why don't I try to be assertive?
- Why do I explain myself to others when I do?
- Why do I consider my worth is based on others' thoughts about me?
- Why do I compare myself with others when I do?
- Why do I lie to myself when I do?
- Why do I waste time with addictions when I do?
- Why do I fall in an illusion of progress when I work on something?

If you question yourself right now, and you answer 100% truthfully, can you truly answer these questions? If I ask you to pursue your answers even further by asking '*but why?*' to every answer you give for about three to five times, can you still answer your own questions? If the answer is no, then it is time to start finding out who you are.

EGO. You have an idea of who you *think* you are, and that is because of your sense of self-importance. Ego is the obstacle that stops you from actually getting to know your true self, *who you can be*. A bad ego is a comfort zone that pulls you into a delusional bubble where you think that you're enough (respectfully), and that illusion doesn't allow true growth and effort to occur. Ego doesn't want to change, it likes itself, so you *have* to admit truthfully to yourself that you have no idea what you're doing for true growth to occur, because one step of healing is realising that you're sick, and thus in pursuing your true self you must realise that you do not know who you truly are.

We all start with the same stats before we discover ourselves: we are young, impulsive, ignorant, indomitable even. Most times we don't even realise our flaws until we stumble upon an individual that brings them to our attention, and even then it usually isn't enough to trigger the necessary response that initiates growth (because of the first stage of competence).

Just because you know what foods you like doesn't mean that you know who you are. You find out who you are when you ask questions that end up being answered with '*I don't know*'. Do you know the questions that needs asking? Use the ones in this chapter until you find yours.

ILLUSTRATE

I get in a fight with my best friend about some stupid youngling things. He assumes some stuff and I assume some too, there is cursing and yelling and whatnot. We both decide on dropping the idea and continuing another day. I get angrier and angrier with every step towards my place, and I just can't shake it off: 'if only he wasn't so stubborn and impulsive and stupid all the time!'. I get to a point where I can't wait to get home and punch some walls when something in my mind changes, for reasons unknown to me even to this day: *I question the reason of our fight*, something I never did before.

I understand the fight itself, but I don't understand *why* we started fighting. What was the reason, where did it go wrong? I continue by breaking the fight in smaller pieces, and I eventually find the culprit that started the fight, which was none other than *'assuming'*. I realised in that moment that both me and my best friend made some assumptions about things that we didn't actually knew the truth about, only our prejudice.

There is nothing to be won from not questioning your moves, your behaviour. Based on this, take a second to ask yourself: 'what is there to gain from engaging in behaviour which's aim is less than noble?'. Answer truthfully before jumping to the next section.

REWARD

Regret. Regret for the vices we displayed, for not knowing better, for the pointless fights, for the wasted moments, for the bonds we lost.

If we truly understand *Hic Et Nunc* (Latin for 'here and now'), then we know that the present is all that we have. The past is gone, and the future hasn't arrived. With this realisation comes a horrible, but beautiful truth: that the moments we have right now will never come back, and because we go only once through a day, that the choice we make will be final for that day. We can be virtuous, or we can be vicious, but not both.

That is why I said in the *Author's note* section that, although as a kid I wouldn't search for a book with the topic I write about, I do realise the importance of teaching someone these lessons. I wish I had the mind I have right now back when I was 15, the mind that knows these lessons because life would've been better. Maybe people I still care about would still be in my life, maybe I would've had courage in moments where I should've done something, maybe I wouldn't have wasted so much time on useless thoughts. Maybe…

That is why we must be better, why we must be noble, why we must question our behaviour, rectify our flaws, and correct our mistakes. Although I believe to be at peace with my past thanks to being grateful (more in the *Guilt & Gratitude* chapter), I do realise that I never want to have regret for my memories again. I want to live life to the fullest, I want to respect my *HIC ET NUNC* tattoo, and I want to be virtuous. The way to do that is to make sure that I focus on what I can control, and that is to choose to make myself better by understanding my behaviour!

ANALYSE

I contact a friend of mine and I ask him what he thinks about *'assuming'*. I get the answer and my life changes for the better, forever. That day I opened my eyes and realised how blind we are as a species. How we take things at face-value and how we don't even *question what we don't understand*. How we just listen to answer, and not to understand. I believe that in my anger I got to a point where my brain had the choice to either get an aneurysm, or to let me in on a little secret, and that secret was to *question everything* that happened so I don't pop. In doing so I managed to not only focus away from the anger that built up, but to also analyse objectively.

Upon breaking the discussion in smaller pieces I found the culprit, *'assuming'*, and I pursued everything with the *'but why?'* behaviour: 'but why did I assume?' until I got to a point where my answer was **'I do not know'**. That was my final answer. The answer that allowed me to realise that I unconsciously believed that I knew who I was until I didn't anymore.

'If I don't know why I'm acting like that, but I absolutely know that I wouldn't choose to act as disrespectfully as I just did, then there must be something going on', I said. That answer started the process of discovering my true self, and dissolving my ego.

UNDERSTAND

Just like one of the aforementioned annoying kids, I start asking *'but why did that happen?'*. Questioning allows the creative process that leads to understanding to start, but because I stopped being an annoying little kid that asks *'but why?'*, I lost my ability to realise that *I don't actually understand anything*. I started listening to my ego and its massive library of information and believing it, never questioning its irrevocable answers and support. I could've picked a totally different route and just think that my best friend is stupid or something, but I took things objectively. I looked at the flow of action and I questioned my actions first, before his. Look at the following picture in order to get an idea of how my brain works. The train of thoughts start at the bottom of the page with the 'I fight with my best friend' line.

BUT WHY?
Question, Understand, Act!

Look at the maze below. This is what went through my head
after the confrontation i had with my best friend. I questioned my behaviour
and i tried to be as unbiased as i could in order to reach a true answer.
I did not want to live in anger my entire life, i knew that i had to change,
so i started by looking deep within me and questioning my behaviour.

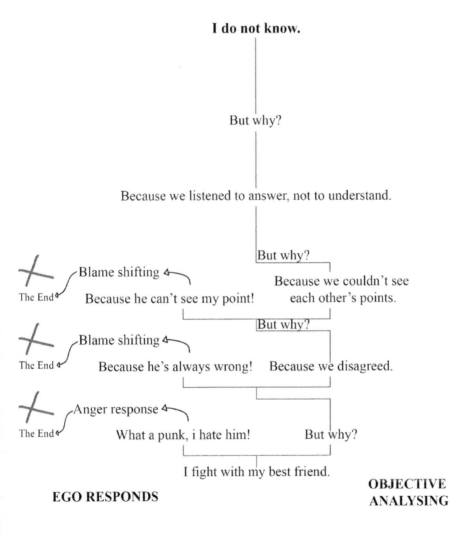

I do not know.

But why?

Because we listened to answer, not to understand.

But why?

Blame shifting
The End   Because he can't see my point!

Because we couldn't see
each other's points.

But why?

Blame shifting
The End   Because he's always wrong!   Because we disagreed.

Anger response
The End   What a punk, i hate him!   But why?

I fight with my best friend.

EGO RESPONDS

**OBJECTIVE
ANALYSING**

You must categorise your behaviour in 'noble' and 'not noble', and after looking at your actions and determining whether they have done harm or not, to question those who have done harm with the 'but why?' system. Check if your actions would be something the person who you want to be would do.

To explain it like I'm talking to a genius five year old: 'Do you want to be a mean person? No? Then why did you assume? Only a mean person would not allow someone to explain themselves. To compound that, if you assume and you know it's wrong, and on top of that you know that it won't lead to your main objective [that of transforming yourself from *who you are* in *who you want to be* (which is a noble person)], why do it?'. Answer, and then question *'but why?'*, three to five times. Now replace 'assume' with a character flaw you have.

OVERCOME

'Great, so what exactly do you want me to do?', you ask. I want you to start looking at your behaviour. Especially at the type of behaviour that isn't noble, the behaviour you have when you don't focus on the things you can control: when you assume, when you say 'yes' even though you want to say 'no', when you compare yourself to someone, when you lie to yourself, when you allow yourself to get mad, basically *whenever something irritates you*.

First of all, *you need to realise that your behaviour is systemized, and that this system is put in place by your library of information (ignorance)*. Whenever you do something, you do it according to some rules you have in your library. Your library of information, unless worked upon continuously to update it, is managed by your ego. Remember that the ego is the sum of information you have accumulated in your life-span, be it your likes and dislikes, your reaction to stimuli, etc.

Second of all, *you must realise that this behaviour is possibly flawed. It is a very important step. You must realise that it is possibly impolite, it is not noble (awareness)*. Nobody likes someone who keeps assuming, who has leaps in judgement, who compares everything (themselves included), who lies to themselves, who gets mad, basically nobody likes to be around someone who complains all the time.

Third of all, *you must question this behaviour using the 'but why?' system (learning)*. As we mentioned in the previous chapter, we get to find ourselves in a predicament when we focus on the things we can't control, but life starts to be good again when we pick ourselves up and we decide to make a change. Thus, you must ask yourself honestly what specific trigger from a situation made you turn towards one of those dishonourable behaviours where you assumed, where you became passive or aggressive (not assertive), where you lied to yourself, where you allowed yourself to get mad. Remember the picture from page 82 and use it as reference. The problem always starts within us!

Lastly, *you must engage in behaviour that spring from your 'noble actions' behaviour. That must become your second nature (mastering).* As I said before, your actions should be categorised in 'noble' and 'not noble'. Your duty is to make sure to engage in as many 'noble actions' as possible (I'm not saying you should start donating to charity everything you own, I'm talking about asking someone for the bigger picture before responding, or choosing to not get mad instead of losing your composure).

Having said all of that, let's look at the introspective questions and answer them:

Why should I question everything? If I manage to stop seeing things at face-value what will that realisation produce? What are the virtues that I will gain from questioning everything? What is my mission?

I should question everything because *things are not always what they seem to be*. We are supposed to listen to understand, not to listen to answer. That is why it is said that knowledge speaks, and wisdom listens. We should always look at things objectively and with the purpose of understanding and learning, and that's because *we do not know the truth about anything to begin with, only our prejudice*. Our ego, our sense of self-importance is a comfortable behaviour that will lead us to ruin if allowed to continue holding the steering-wheel of our lives. Thus, we should question everything so that our ego doesn't think for us, but that instead we think for ourselves, and consequently to develop our sense of deeper understanding that ultimately leads to character development.

Understanding this lesson produces one very important realisation: that I do not know who I am. In questioning matter, we allow ourselves to think outside of the box and to grasp the subtle substance, the subtle message that *we do not know why we do some things that we do*. We do not know why we assume, why we get angry, or why we think the way we think about something that makes us uncomfortable, or comfortable for the matter. But we can reach an understanding if we follow the hierarchical thread using the '*but why?*' system.

The virtues that I will gain from questioning everything are prudence, justice, and temperance. This is a beautiful domino effect where not only do you question something and try to look at it objectively, which helps by thinking honestly about yourself and realising your mistakes, but you also gain a deeper understanding of *who you want to be* and *who you currently aren't*. If we realise we lied, and we know we don't want to be liars, we immediately correct ourselves. Thus, in discovering your flaw (the culprit that initiated the anger or ruined the experience) and correcting it, you are now on the path that leads to *who you want to be*.

My mission is to categorise behaviour in 'noble' and 'not noble', and to look at my actions from now on with the intent of pursuing only those that are noble, only those that *someone who I want to be would do*.

Thus, we can conclude that by looking at our behaviour objectively, as through the eyes of a stranger, and *questioning our feelings, thoughts, and actions,* we can reach a deeper understanding of who we want to be. We want to be better, and we want to fix our flaws and possible shortcomings too. Nobody likes suffering and that is why we must focus on understanding ourselves and our faults. The more we correct about ourselves, the happier we get!

What to take away: Whenever you have an uneasy feeling just question yourself *'but why do I feel like this?'*. Allow yourself to pursuit everything objectively by breaking down the situation into smaller fragments until you get to the culprit. *'But why?'* is the way to ultimately healing yourself.

Chapter 2
WELCOME YOUR DARKNESS

A rabbit isn't virtuous, it just can't do anything except get eaten.
— JORDAN B. PETERSON

PURPOSE

The purpose of this chapter is to bring to attention that burying our emotions doesn't kill them, but instead it offers them power over us. Burying emotions is equal to not questioning them, and not questioning stems from the ego's control over the inspecting function, as mentioned in the previous chapter.

INTROSPECTIVE

This chapter and the next one pertains the most to my existence, and are written from the soul. All of my life I dealt with angry people who assume everything and question nothing, that have a know-it-all attitude. We must increase the limit of our composure by removing the ego, and prevent logic from being overwhelmed by our emotions. The way to do that is by acknowledging and accepting that we are hurt when we get hurt, and *understanding why* we are hurt. Thus, we ask ourselves:

Why should I understand my emotions? If I manage to understand my emotions, what will that realisation produce? What are the virtues that I will gain from understanding my emotions? What is my mission?

DEFINE

What are *emotions*? *Emotions* are **temporary** states brought on by neurophysiological changes. As happiness is brought on by the activation of the frontal lobe (more in the *Happiness is the journey, not the destination* chapter), so is anxiety brought on by the excessive use of the adrenal glands. In layman terms, emotions are feelings we have that are generated by the choices we or someone else make.

We are fortunate enough to be the pillars of a new era. A new era where we have an online library that everyone can access and benefit from, we have new clinical research for major branches such as psychology and medicine, we have virtual worlds, artificial intelligence, everything simplified and made for our comfort. In spite of that, I look at the people around me and realise that they still have anger, still have an unnecessary arrogance, still have a despisable delusional superiority in their lexicon and body language. I realise that, although the world seems to change, individuals don't, and that is where the problem is. To truly change the world we need to change ourselves, to change as individuals, as clicheic as it sounds. So what seems to be their problem (besides inflation, taxes, and whatever shortages that kill us slowly)?

I believe the problem can be explained with an old Japanese quote. It is said that people have three masks. The first they show to the world, the second they show to their close friends, and the third they show to no one. If you think about it, our inter-humane relationships are always based on these three masks: when we meet someone, we do our best to behave and to show our good side, as opposed to the relaxed behaviour we show when we are with our best friend. We try to live separate lives that have contrasting gears we shift in. We are rudely honest with our friends, and politely dishonest with strangers because we wish to avoid a confrontation. But this isn't good, because it usually leads to denial.

ILLUSTRATE

Having a brother is vital because you have double the experience gained from life. I have three people that I think about as brothers of mine, and I went through thick and thin with this one. Today I will illustrate something that is the sum of a lot of years and practice, so don't worry if you don't get it right by first try. There will come a day where you will understand that some things just need time, no matter how much we want to hurry them (the four stages of competence).

This is a recent occurrence. My brothers and I are playing a toxic game called League of Legends ever since 2015, and in this game we are five players against five. Yesterday we were in a game mode called ARAM (all random all mid) where the two teams of five champions each meet on a single lane map. This map has four towers, and the purpose is to defend yours and destroy theirs with the help of minions.

The champions have levels, abilities, and an ultimate ability (a skill that has a long cooldown and inflicts big damage). We were in the middle of the map, at our first tower. We reach level 6, get our ultimate abilities, use them, and continue hitting minions and dealing damage to the enemy team whilst our ultimate abilities recharge.

Since every ultimate has different cooldowns, some people recharge theirs faster than others. That can be tracked in the bottom right corner. There, the icons of your team's colleagues are displayed, big and obvious, and you can see their ultimate status (and even click on it to see how many seconds left until fully recharged), alongside their health and status (alive or dead).

Here's the fun part: we were talking on voice chat. One of my bros jumps in the enemy team with his ultimate ability, dies, and then asks us what we're doing, and why we didn't jump in. I tell him that my ultimate isn't ready. He says that that's the reason we are speaking on voice chat (something like 'why didn't you inform me?'). I tell him that he can't accuse me of that exactly because we're on voice chat, and he neither checked if my ultimate is ready, nor did he inform us that he's going in. How can I help him if he doesn't ask for help? Why (and how) does he get mad and push the blame on others for the choices he didn't take (his own choices)?

There is nothing to be won from losing your cool. Based on this, take a second to ask yourself: 'what is there to gain from losing my temper?'. Answer truthfully before jumping to the next section.

REWARD

Anger. Anger is the reward we get from losing our temper.

When was the last time you got angry? Do you remember why you got angry? *Are you still angry right now, or do you realise that that emotion passed?* Now that you're calm and you think about it, did the situation you were in got fixed because you got angry? Did a solution magically appear? Did you getting angry accomplish that which you hoped to? If my crystal ball is right, the solution didn't appear, the problem didn't get fixed, and all you did was get angry.

So if getting angry, raising your voice, throwing stuff and whatnot isn't fixing your problem, then why not try to look at yourself and see what got you angry? Why not use the *'but why?'* system to understand your emotions? Look for that inside of you which got you angry, question yourself truthfully about what it is, and realise that it is something you have control over to change!

Realise that in life there are always two options: a positive and a negative, a yes and a no, a do and a don't. You can always choose to have an opinion, or choose not to. You can always choose to have expectations, or choose not to. You can always choose to get mad, or choose not to. But to do that, you must realise that the behaviour of getting mad is neither noble, nor does it lead to *who you want to be*, nor does it solve anything, and since it springs from within you, only you can make yourself get mad.

ANALYSE

My brother focused on the things he can't control: that we should make his choices for him in his place, and driven by his ego, he tried to push the blame on 'external forces' when the actual reason for why he got mad was a result of his choices. But we are not others' secretaries, and we don't have to take others' choices for them.

Instead of focusing on the things he can control: checking our ultimate cooldown status, informing us that he wants to engage in a fight, etc., he just straight up went in-between the enemy team, died, and blamed it on us. When confronted about that, he shifted the blame on the fact that we're on voice chat, and that we should've informed him. I then informed him that I cannot take his decisions for him, and that next time he'd better check our ultimate abilities cooldown and inform us when he is ready to engage, since 'we are on voice chat', instead of blaming us for his actions, or lack thereof.

UNDERSTAND

One thing I wish to stress: not all people are good. Just as we have the potential of evil in us, so too do others. There are truly malevolent people out there. Do not confuse nobility for being devoid of evil. This can lead to waking up one day and realising that your entire life is a lie as a result of doing something bad in an uncontrollable impulse, something you didn't think it was possible to do since you believed yourself to be only good. Just pointing that out.

We know we cannot control our emotions, but we can understand them, and if we understand them then we can control our actions. That is why it is very important to confront our fears and to *actively reflect* on what we felt in confrontational moments. It is important to know our triggers, to know what makes us flip the switch and bring out the anger, and by using the *'but why?'* system we can hierarchically pursue the thread of thoughts that lead from calmness to anger, we can discover what exact part of our judgement triggered that response, and then we can fix it.

If you allow yourself to think about all the times you got angry, you will realise how you're just like a self-driving car following the instructions of a GPS device. It is always the same behaviour that yields the same results, it is always the same illusion that we are in control when we aren't. But a *good*, qualified driver can regain control of a car that is in peril, and so too can you take control of your actions when you are in 'peril', but do you have the driving license to do so? Are you a *good* driver? Do you know the moves you need to make to stabilise your vehicle?

The reason I'm asking this is because it is easier to hurt the other than it is to understand them, and it's so easy to understand why: as mentioned before, ego is the sense of self-importance that is necessary to assemble your character traits, your wishes, your likes and dislikes, your life goal, and your motivation until you're ready to wake up.

Briefly put, ego is the hoarding of information. The information is cherished since it's the only thing of value to itself. Like a lioness protecting her cub, so too will the ego do whatever is possible to retaliate and protect if its information is contradicted (someone disagrees with us), *because the ego is always right*. The ego can't accept that the only thing it has (information) is being taken away because then it is powerless, it has no value, *it dies since the sense of self-importance that believes itself and only itself to be right cannot exist at the same time as a sense of believing others to be right*. That is why you must dissolve your ego, and only when you truly understand that fact will you truly start living instead of existing, and know *who you want to be.*

Going back to the subject of masks, I believe that the behaviour of burying our emotions and trying to be politely dishonest, as opposed to *understanding our emotions and politely confronting people* is a big problem of this century. Denial means to not accept the truth. Denial is the shift of *blaming ourselves for being weak and failing to defend ourselves* to *blaming the others for hurting us*. It is the refusal to accept the truth that we are in a predicament because of our fault, generally speaking. Mr. Peterson says that *a rabbit isn't virtuous, it just can't do anything except get eaten* (chapter quote), and this goes so well with the contrast between the rabbit and the wolf.

There is a quote that is very dear to me that says 'the lion might be stronger, but the wolf doesn't perform at the circus'. Many people nowadays believe that they are virtuous by not harming anyone, that by not defending themselves (and therefore avoiding conflict) they are good people, but that is not the case. Being defenceless does not equal being virtuous. I believe that to be virtuous is to have the potential to do evil, but to choose not to. To cause no harm, but to take no harm either. To question your behaviour, to control your actions, to control your power, to become the wolf. The other option is to be the rabbit. To be the sheep that follows the herd blindly and without questioning the direction.

A lot of people consider themselves lions or tigers, big bad strong entities with unlimited power, but all they are is puppets that jump the hoop when they're told to jump the hoop. But the wolf is a free animal. A free thinker. It knows its power and that is why it doesn't go to the circus. You have to be the wolf, you have to know your power. To be a bit plainer and to numb down the metaphorical speeches, *you must question and understand your emotions*, for only when you master them do you master yourself.

OVERCOME

'Great, so how do we accept our darkness and understand our emotions?', you ask. You already know: you realise that you shouldn't focus on that which you can't control!

Most of the times we get angry because we have something to prove to the world, and because of that we allow no one to have an opinion about something we think, about something we like, about something we try to be. In which category does this exact type of behaviour fit in? This behaviour fits in the category of focusing on that which you can't control.

The best course of action is to realise that everyone is allowed to have a disrespectful opinion, and even if they shouldn't, that you have no power to decide whether they do or not, only the power to be affected by it or not. Their opinions only angers you because you let it anger you. It only angers you because you think that it will shape your judgement, so realise now that their opinion has no power to change your judgement, only you do!

People have the right to speak, and you have the right to listen to understand, see if what they say is the wisdom of a great mind or the fear of a tiny one, and move on. You also have the right to get up and leave. Their opinion shouldn't affect you if your behaviour is morally correct and justified. You will sleep the same tonight, you will pursue your purpose the same, you will live the same, with or without their opinion. Let them talk, and you carry on with your life and your practice, and see where you both get to be in five years. Sometimes others' 'hurtful' opinions allows us to wake up and realise that we're stepping on that which we said we respect, but first we need to think of their opinions as critiques, not attacks. As something to learn from if there is something to be learned from, not as an insult. Remember this!

In order to flood a boat you need to have a hole, but you can't have a hole if you don't make one in the first place. So the steps to avoid making a hole are as follows:

First of all, *you must realise that just like you, everyone has control over their mind, over their ability to create opinions, and over their ability to express them. According to justice, you must respect everyone's rights, including the right to opinion.* However, nowadays everyone has something to say, and it isn't necessarily smart, so there lies your satisfaction! Just because someone says something it doesn't necessarily mean it's smart. So to expect people to not hurt you is a painful trait that springs from both the fact that you can't defend yourself (rabbit), and from the fact that you're focusing on what you can't control (trying to control their opinions). Let them say what they have to say and realise that, since you can't control their opinions, there's no reason to bother. And if you shouldn't bother since you can't control their opinions, then why complain about them? Do you complain about the colour of the sky? And even if you do, does the sky change its colour? You can either cry about it, or you can accept it, and that's how you defend yourself and get strong.

Second of all, *you must realise that opinions are words, and since words have no weight to them, you shouldn't be hurt by them unless they are true*. Realise how people cannot magically bind you. People's words are not magic spells that once uttered bind you in place, unable to move. They are not obstacles. They could say that the sun is blue and that your skirt is ugly and you'd still be able to take a step forward. Why? Because they're just words, not magical binding spells. They have no control over your choice to do what you plan on doing! If you're happy doing what you're doing (and it's moral), then you're already living a better life than them (respectfully).

Third of all, *you must realise that in life it is not your words that talk, but your actions. Words are just that: words*. They are only a verbal representation of what you believe in, but actions show if you really believe what you say. Behind words there is no weight. There is no sweat, no hard work. All of that hard work can be found in actions, and those who have time to give opinions are not busy enough with their lives, and that says something about them!

Lastly, *realise that you do not exist to impress people*. You live for yourself, you live to be happy for yourself, and you try to be better for yourself. There's no purpose in being healthier and happier than another, but there is purpose in being healthier and happier than yesterday. Think about it! If what you're doing is right and researched, then getting mad is not a result of knowing yourself to be wrong, but a result of your necessity to prove yourself with words, and not with actions. But why is that?

Maybe because you're afraid some words will steal your happiness. Maybe because you haven't learned to think 15 minutes in the future, haven't learned to think that you will still be on your way to do that which you proposed to do, regardless if a dog barked at you or not. Think about all the times you had an argument and got mad. You still went ahead and did your choirs, your task, your job, your gym, or whatever you were supposed to do that day, right? Just with some extra anger added to your cup. The dog's barking didn't stop you from achieving what you planned on doing, but your decision to think of its bark as offensive about what you planned to do will definitely try to stop you from doing it. That is why it is important to believe in yourself (fortitude).

Withal, maybe you get angry because you are not living the philosophy you preach, because if you truly believed in yourself, then you knew that **saying something says nothing, but doing something says something**! Why stop and prove yourself to everyone who doesn't believe in you with words and waste your time. Do you know how many people don't believe in you? It'd take you more time than you have in your life to explain with words to each and every one why what you're doing is right and why they're wrong for being rude, when you could prove yourself to the whole world at the same time by excelling at that which you proposed on doing.

Why? *Because actions matter, not words*! If you pass by a gate where a dog barks, you probably look at it and continue on your way, so why would you put your heart in the words of others, especially in the hands of a stranger who doesn't know you, your worth, your sweat & tears, your hard work? Realise that a dog's barking is just that, a bark, empty words. Words don't stand in your way, they doesn't restrict your movement, they don't take away your ability to go ahead and do what you plan on doing. They are just words. Whenever you get threatened by someone's words know that you are to blame, because you give those words power over you **by not trusting in your potential!** In understanding that lies the secret that, when you research what you do, the only one who can stop yourself is yourself. No amount of barks can stop a train that is led by a determined conductor!

Having said all that, let's look at the introspective questions and to answer them:

Why should I understand my emotions? If I manage to understand my emotions what will that realisation produce? What are the virtues that I will gain from understanding my emotions? What is my mission?

I should understand my emotions in order to better control myself. Trying to logically pursue your train of thoughts in an argument when you get disturbed by your emotions is the same as trying to study when you're disturbed by background noise. But if you allow yourself today, tomorrow, next month, and the next years to actively focus when you get in that tense situation, to ask yourself *'but why am I getting angry?'*, and to try to understand the culprit, I promise you that you will have a better life.

The realisation that will be produced after acknowledging that I must understand my emotions will be that I am now actually closer to being in control of my actions. If someone challenges me by stating something negative about something I appreciate, I can now focus on the fact that I am getting slightly negative. Once I realise that I am getting angry I must now question *'but why am I getting negative?'*, and to truthfully answer. We can get angry because someone made a point about something and we want to defend it since we believe in it, or maybe because we stupidly made an imaginary statue of someone we respect and they shamed that person, or maybe because they like to tease or to bully**, or maybe because we cannot simply understand that everyone is entitled to an opinion and that we don't need to change it, not with words at least**. Now what is our course of action? Our action must depend on the situation itself:

- If we are dealing with a bully that only tries to get to us, we must realise that our worth is not decided by them, but by us. We are free to enjoy and to pursue whatever we desire, for we only live once and we are not here to impress anyone. Thus, the problem is not us, and we shouldn't explain anything and waste any more time, for it will fall on deaf ears. Do not give pearls to swine.
- On the other hand, if we are dealing with someone who is genuinely interested in carrying out a debate in a specific domain, then we should engage positively. We should put aside our ego and listen to

understand, not to answer. There is always another point of view, that which you cannot see from your perspective, and consequently information to gain.

The virtues that I will gain from understanding emotions are justice, fortitude, and temperance.

My mission is to focus on the things that anger me when they anger me. To realise that the only thing I have control over is my choices, and that my perception of things is an extension of my mind. I must realise that the thing that angers me comes from my perception, and I need to question it and see where the flaw is. It can be something as banal as getting irritated because I spilled water on me, or as grave as wanting to hurt someone because they accidently wronged me. Everything starts from our behaviour, from our judgement, and just as anger is a weapon we can use if we master it, so too it is a weapon people can use against us if we don't master it.

To conclude, realise that in life we all have purposes, and that the only thing that can stand in our way are physical things. Boxes. Walls. Fences. Broken bridges. Traffic. Also realise that even those can only stop your body, not your mind. Your mind can only be stopped by an opinion if you let it, because otherwise an opinion isn't a physical object that can block you from doing what you planned on doing. Only you can stop yourself, so stop taking actions based on your temporary emotions, and instead let your actions dictate your emotions!

Just because people can't see the truth doesn't mean you have to deal with it. If you tried explaining it and nothing sticks, move on.

What to take away: Someone who angers you can only anger you if you allow it. If you ask yourself *'why am I getting angry?'* and pursue the train of thoughts truthfully in order to find the flaw and fix it, then you're already better than you were yesterday, and more capable to confront situations in a more logic and composed state due to your newfound control. Focus on listening to understand, not to answer, even with yourself.

FOREGONE

Chapter 3
STOP ASSUMING

If you assume the worst, you disappoint someone. If you assume the best, you disappoint yourself. If you do not assume, you see the truth.
— DANTE SAPATINAS

PURPOSE

The purpose of this chapter attempts to bring to attention that assuming is nothing but disappointment, unless you're a math teacher. It is a vice that will end up hurting either you or someone else, and the sooner you realise that there is more happiness in questioning and understanding than there is in simply believing what your ego is feeding you, the faster you'll better yourself!

INTROSPECTIVE

Assuming is a combination of multiple vices. It is a lack of care, because if we actually cared we would ask in order to expand our knowledge about the subject (prudence). It is a lack of character, because if we truly knew ourselves we would use our brain instead of being rude to the other and letting our ego decide that our prejudice is enough (justice). It is a lack of control, for if we understood our emotions we wouldn't try to hurt the other one just because we felt hurt by something they did or said (temperance). Generally speaking, assuming is wrong and this chapter will highlight why, but first let's go ahead and look at this chapter's questions:

FOREGONE

Why should I not assume? If I manage to stop assuming, what will that realisation produce? What are the virtues that I will gain from not assuming? What is my mission?

DEFINE

What is *assuming*? *Assuming* is a making a statement based on little or no evidence at all. In this specific context, *assuming* is an arrogant prejudice that makes us believe we know why someone acts the way they do, be it that we think we know why they're saying something or doing something, *but not being really sure*. It is a leap in judgement that makes us think we know the answer to someone else's actions based on surface-level behaviour, and it stems from the inability to realise that we should question, and not give in to our prejudice, that we should listen to understand, and not to simply reply.

Being a statement based on little to no evidence at all, it is a mistake to assume and take things for granted in life, and this mistake is born from the failure to realise that we can't control anything besides our choices. How many times did we assume that something will work in our favour, and it didn't?

The focus of this chapter will be on conflict that arises because of our mistakes. We cannot control other people and situations, so we must focus on what we can control, which is ourselves by *'not confronting someone without giving them the chance to explain themselves'* and *'not taking things for granted'*. Not only is this noble, but it also allows us to grow.

One life rule that I fixate on is: do not let your emotions dictate your actions, let your actions dictate your emotions. You cannot control your emotions, that we understand, but you can control your actions, and identical to nausea, you can choose to either go to the bathroom, or to go right then and there on you and your mates. The choice is yours.

ILLUSTRATE

I have so many moments in my life where I assumed that it is hard to pick one:

- I once assumed that a company will actually call me back next month because they said they're waiting for some papers, so I took a loan of £300 from a friend with the promise that I'll pay next month. They never called so I paid the following year (taking things for granted).
- I once assumed that treating someone like a can of tuna and giving them a certain date and time after which they can't contact me anymore was a good way to push them. It wasn't (trying to control others' feelings).
- One of the worst ones is when someone assumes something about you that you neither did nor said, and when you confront them about it they get defensive and use the banal 'I'm only kidding'. We all know at least one person like that (I don't know what that is, just know to stay away from it).

There is nothing to be won from trying to guess the amount of choices someone made that lead to them saying or doing something that didn't resonate well with your logic. What if you don't have the full picture? Based on this, take a second to ask yourself: 'what is there to gain from believing that I can guess all the choices a person made that lead to the behaviour I declared offensive?'. Answer truthfully before jumping to the next section.

REWARD

Disappointment. That is the reward. You end up having remorse, and disappointment thereafter. You think that you can understand someone's behaviour, that which they say or do, but forget four important things:

- That life is not white or black, but grey, and only the perception we have from our perspective gives it colour.
- That we can always change our perspective by asking someone what they mean with their behaviour, and gain deeper comprehension of a subject.
- That behind a behaviour there are a multitude of choices that made that behaviour happen.
- That we cannot control the avalanche of choices that we made in our lives, so why try to control or guess another's?

About yourself: When you look at your actions, you can get mad when you have false perceptions and expectations about yourself. It all starts with an error you make in the 'equation' you use to calculate your actions: how do you plan on being successful today, on completing that report, on achieving that marathon personal record, on not fighting anyone, on not feeling depressed, and on being in a good mood when your diet consists of only carb-coma foods (you know the postprandial somnolence), when you smoke, when you drink, when you go to bed late, when you do all those actions that negatively stress your nervous system (more about this in *The Nervous System* chapter)? Why do you assume that you will do your best today, when you're currently dragging yourself on the floor, and get disappointed after having false expectations? There's nothing wrong with trying your best, don't get me wrong, but don't assume based on false expectations! Better yet, don't assume and don't have expectations, instead give it your best and accept what it is, not what you want it to be!

About others: When you look at someone's actions, especially someone who is close to you, and you allow your perception of that person's apparent behaviour to get inside your head, you can get angry. Being angry can make you search for things that aren't there, and do things you wouldn't normally do. Think about something as banal as living with someone (flatmates), and waking up in the morning and realising that the fast-food leftovers are gone. Although this is a specific, isolated case, it can happen. You can pick up the phone and send repulsive messages, only to find out afterwards that they had an overnight guest, and that the guest ate the leftovers. ***The problem isn't who ate the food, it's that you assumed and that you didn't research.***

Not only did you blame the wrong person on the assumption that, if only you two live there, there couldn't have been someone else who ate them, but you also focused on that which you can't control: crying over the past instead of realising that you should've split the leftovers that night. No sir, you left it all together, unlabelled, and without declaring a part. ***The problem always starts from focusing on what you can't control***, which is not declaring your share, not realising that the food is already gone and no amount of complaining will bring it back, ***instead of focusing on what you can control***, which is asking your flatmate about what happened to the food (maybe it got stinky, maybe it leaked and had to be thrown away), awaiting the answer, and realising that, even if they replied that they ate it, you couldn't go ahead and ask why they didn't think about keeping you some. Why? Because you made your choice the night before! You made your choice to not split food, to not declare it! You can't expect others to take your choices for you, you can't expect others to know if you want some or not, to keep you some from the goodness of their heart, to label a part of it as your part and to put it safe. You have to take action and say 'this mine, no touchy!'. Now you know what to do next time: don't complain, use your brain!

ANALYSE

Assuming comes in different forms:

- You can assume that it's okay to confront someone about something that you saw but have no backstory on, *'but why do you want to do that without knowing the entire story?'* (Not everything is what it seems)
- You can aggressively confront someone about something you heard, *'but why not tell them what you know and ask if it is true?'* (Don't give in to your prejudice)
- You can assume that you will get that promotion you always wanted and end up disappointed if you don't, so *'why assume and take for granted?'* (Don't take things for granted)
- You can assume that your date might go bad and cancel, *'but what if it doesn't and you lose an opportunity because you assumed wrong?'* (Don't focus on what you can't control)

UNDERSTAND

Assuming is nothing but a vice. Our ego feeds us an over-inflated-self-importance-sense that leads us to search for others like us to gang up on those who seem weak. We make school gangs and we prey on the weak, we look at someone and the way they walk, talk, and act, and instantly assume that they must be this or that because of this and that, without asking them if what we believe is actually true (not that it's any of our business).

'Why would we ask them if we have everything right in front of us?', says our ego. We dress rich but our life is poor, because the way others perceive us and their assumption that we are out of their league feeds our ego, but why is that? Is it because we actually have nothing to show to the world and we distract ourselves from that ugly reality? We have no quality, nothing interesting going on in our life, no life ambition so we're hungry for some appreciation? Are we actually looking for love and pleasure wherever we can, and get it whenever we can? But dressing rich and taking the bus is such a big contrast…respectfully.

Regardless of what type of assuming you engage in, be it either to believe something untrue about someone, to think someone wanted to hurt you purposefully, to blindly dive in that credit card because your boss said the promotion *might* be yours, or any other type of assuming, you must understand two things:

- The fact that you need to look at a situation and to question yourself: 'based on what information do I believe this? Is it prejudice or do I have facts?'
- The fact that you never know the truth about anything, you only know the prejudice you have! Please allow yourself next time you catch yourself in the act of assuming to ask yourself truthfully three to five times 'but why do I think this/believe this?'.

If you do this you'll see that we get to a point where we don't understand how life functions anymore, we just know it does, but in order to get to that point we need to wish to understand *and to also pursue understanding actively* (first stage of competence). We can't do that when we assume because assuming is prejudice, and prejudice is a false belief, a belief that is not based on actual reality and research. Too many times we take things at face-value, ***too many times we think that the way we see things are the way things actually are, and the way we feel about someone is how they actually are***, but that is nothing but a reflection of our EGO! Assuming is the shifting of blame, the pointing of fingers, it's thinking that all problems are external, not caused by us, when this is nowhere further from the truth! All problems in our life are caused by us and our choices, and the faster you understand this the faster you can wake up and change your life!

OVERCOME

'So what can I do to make sure I don't assume?', you ask.

First of all, *we need to realise that we do not know anything about anything, only our prejudice.* We can only put two and two together to reach four, but maybe the answer isn't four anymore, maybe something happened in that equation. Maybe the plan you had with your mates changed, and they didn't inform you (for whatever reason). So a change of plan is a new plan, and the answer isn't four anymore, it's five! Or maybe the answer was never four, and because you lacked the entire story since you only read the first part of the equation without checking the back-page, you assumed that it must be four since you only had two and two on the first page, and missed a couple of two's on the back-page!

Second of all, *we must focus on that which we can control, which is our ability to research.* You can shift blame very easily when you don't focus on what you can control (checking back with them about the plan, making sure you're still on for today, you know, the regular pre-check-up), and if you assume that what was said is what will be without researching, you can get very disappointed and hurt. It takes less than a minute to call someone (that which you can control) and say 'we still up for today?'.

Third of all, *we must not take things for granted.* This is a combination of the first two steps. If you show up at the place and nobody will be there, you will be left with a sour taste in your mouth. You will be angry and shift blame, and probably think 'why didn't they call me, they were my friends, how dare they!'. But that's an error in your judgement! Although it would be nice and 'normal' to do that, it is not their duty to make your choices for you, but yours! It is your duty to focus on what you can control (do a pre-check-up) and to not take for granted that others will do your actions in your stead (people forget, or maybe they posted it on a group where you got notifications muted, or they both thought that the other one will inform you). *They are not your secretary, and even if they were, you must always do your own due-diligence!*

It is your duty, whatever the situation is, to focus on checking the status. To focus on that which you can control. To not look at things and believe that they are what they seem without research, for there can be an avalanche of reasons and choices behind them that lead to that behaviour, an avalanche that you are unaware of! Do you want to feel shame when someone tells you that that's not what is actually going on, and that your perception is wrong and your accusations are wrong too? Your job is to realise that someone who is seemingly bad is only a reflection of your perception, like the woman who steals bread for her child. You see a woman who steals, without knowing that she has a baby, but she sees the only opportunity the world gave her to feed her baby. So which one of you is right? I'd say that, if you want to know the truth, you'd sit down with her and ask her. See her point of view, not only yours.

Now that we understand what assuming is and that hopefully you've had some moments from your life where you assumed pop up in your mind, let's look at the introspective questions and answer them:

Why should I not assume? If I manage to stop assuming, what will that realisation produce? What are the virtues that I will gain from not assuming? What is my mission?

I should not assume because assuming is a combination of the three behaviours mentioned in the previous chapters, behaviours that I am trying to correct:

- I know that it is easier to shift blame than it is to accept that I am wrong, so now I question my actions (prudence).
- I know that it is easier to get angry than it is to calm down and understand my emotions, so for my sake I now try to understand them (fortitude).
- I know that I cannot control what the other person does, but that I can control what my actions are, so I will question, listen, understand what the problem is, and focus only on what I can control (temperance).
- I will allow my actions to dictate my emotions, and I will give the benefit of the doubt to the person in question. If I am the person in question, I will search for the true reason to why I'm assuming by questioning myself if what I know is prejudice or facts, and if I'm not actually shifting the blame by expecting others to do my choices in my stead (justice).

The realisation produced by understanding what assuming is and not engaging in this behaviour anymore will be to be set free from the illusion that I created. From the prison of my own mind, of my own thoughts. Upon understanding that assuming is a 'negative hope' and that, regardless of the positive or negative outcome, the outcome is regret and disappointment, I will be set free. You can either be disappointed because you were right, or disappointed because you were wrong, there's really no victory in assuming. So let all the time wasted, all the negative thoughts and the anxiety be gone with the wind.

The virtues that I will gain from not assuming are justice and temperance!

My mission is to let go of my ego and to understand that *assuming* is not noble:

- When it comes to situations, the reason you assume is because you focus on that which you cannot control: you take for granted situations without checking up on them, and get mad when the others don't play secretary and take choices for you that you should take for yourself. Do your own due-diligence, and stop believing that things are as they seem to be, that your perception of things is the only possible truth! When/because you believe things are as they seem, you don't have a reason to research if those things really are what they seem, and because you never research, you get mad and do things you wouldn't do: you search for answers to invalid questions, you try to justify situations using your limited information and understand why what happened just happened, when actually what you believe happened isn't probably what actually happened. Empty glass of water, + & -.
- You then blame people. You categorise people as 'bad' based on surface-level behaviour that you have no additional information about. You blame people because you don't focus on that which you can control, like asking questions and getting deeper comprehension of a subject.

You focus on that which you cannot control because your ego still has control over your life. The reason your ego has control over your own life is because you believe you know who you are, but that's just a whisper that tempts you to not change (since change is uncomfortable), and a reflection of your lack of nobility, for if you questioned yourself if you are noble in the first place, you wouldn't be controlled by your ego if you realised that your behaviour isn't good, but bad. Because your ego has control over your life, you don't question your behaviour since your ego assures you that you know who you are, and there doesn't need to be an inspection done.

Because there's no inspection done, when you get angry you remain angry and lash out, and have no reason to ask yourself if that is normal and if you should change yourself. Since there's no inspection needed, surely this is what your behaviour is supposed to be like. Since repetition is the mother of learning, and your ego taught you to *'never back down, to know your worth, and to fight for what you know because that is the only thing you have, and others shouldn't take it from you'*, you now fight everyone who has an opposite opinion about you or something you like, say, or do. Because you cannot control yourself and not only do you not want to change, but you focus on controlling others and trying to make them change and revolve around you like you're always correct and the sun of their solar system, you get to assume that it must be their fault that your life is miserable, and that they are stupid and can't understand your point. But do you even *try to understand their point?*.

Thus, don't listen to answer, listen to understand. Calm down when you get angry, and ask yourself: 'what if this is my fault? If I calm down and try to address the situation calmly, what will I learn from this?'.

What to take away: There is no point in assuming other than it being a guilt trap that leads to senseless pain. Focus on your conversation, be civilized, be composed, and listen to the person in order to understand what their *actual* point is, not the one created in your mind by your ego's assumptions. There's no person? Learn about the situation then.

Chapter 4
BE ASSERTIVE

To be passive is to let others decide for you. To be aggressive is to decide for others. To be assertive is to decide for yourself. And to trust that there is enough, that you are enough.
— EDITH EVA EGER

PURPOSE

The purpose of this chapter is to bring to attention that we are negotiators, and that we can't negotiate if we can't say 'no'. Withal, we can't pursue our maximum potential and discover our true worth if we can't say 'no'.

INTROSPECTIVE

*Not saying 'no' can lead to a decrease in our perceived worth because we might do things for others that do not align with **who we want to be***. In order to realise our full potential and worth, we must not be afraid to stand by our choices, even if it means that we might disagree with others. As long as the reason is right, you don't disagree just do disagree, and you can back it up with research if it's the case, all should be right in the world. Thus, let's do our exercise and ask ourselves:

Why should I be assertive? If I manage to be assertive, what will that realisation produce? What are the virtues that I will gain from being assertive? What is my mission?

DEFINE

What does it mean to *be assertive*? To *be assertive* means to know yourself, *and to be yourself (noble)*.

Being assertive means to categorise your actions in actions that *do lead* to who you want to be, and actions that *do not lead* to who you want to be, and to stand by your choice. To realise that you cannot be who you want to be if you always say 'yes' to others, or if you always engage in behaviour that doesn't lead to *who you want to be*.

But, and this is very important, it also means to find a way through which both you and the person you negotiate with can be happy, instead of one being happy at the expense of the other's happiness. A passive person will forfeit their rights and let someone make a choice for them, and an aggressive person will make a choice in someone's stead and abuse their rights.

If a random stranger asks us to give them our car keys for a ride, we'd instantly go past them without thinking twice, but if our best friend asks for the car, we'd be inclined to lend it to them. Based on this we understand that the closer a person is to our heart, the more we are willing to cross some boundaries, to take some actions that we wouldn't, to support someone in spite of what that does or says about us. But what do we do if, although we'd be inclined to do so, we don't want to? Are we bad people if we don't appeal to every request another might have, or is there a limit that needs to be declared?

I believe that a limit should exist, regardless of the status possessed by the person who does the request, and I use this criteria to declare it:

- Is this person a manipulator or a benefactor?
- Is that which they ask of me a necessity or superfluity?
- Am I willing to engage in this behaviour and accept its risks?
- Will this behaviour lead me to *who I want to be*?

ILLUSTRATE

All of my life I've been passive as a result of my hyper positivity. I feel like even today I need nothing from this world, besides health and a device to study. Today I am assertive, don't get me wrong, but only in things I declare as important to me, those which lead to *who I want to be.*

Thus, I present to you the only example I can muster, one that is banal but presents perfectly how to be assertive (and it's not even entirely my example). You see, a couple of years ago I was sharing a house with my mates. We all had our own shelf in the fridge, and our own top cabinet. Every time I bought ingredients, such as olive oil, bread, Nutella, etc., I woke up in the morning with them used. First time I thought to myself that, should the situation reverse and I find myself in their shoes, I would also use them. After all, it was the first time this happened, and it wasn't like they emptied half of each container, maybe they needed some olive oil and bread.

Unfortunately people are rude, and if they notice that they can take more the next day, they will continue to take more. This went on for as long as I let it, I mean after all, *it's only bread, right?* Wrong! It's not about the fact that it's bread, it's about the mechanism behind it, it's that someone is going through my personal stuff, without asking permission, and continues to use my ingredients to the point of depletion. It's about my rights.

Not only was this happening to me, but it was also happening to someone I consider like a brother to me who, ironically, is the one who taught me about assertiveness many years ago.

So what did he do? He messaged the group and asked for a gathering. We met after work and discussed this issue. He said: 'guys, I understand if you want to take some bread. It's only bread, but please do not eat it if you see that there are only two slices left. Just as you have the right to wake up and eat the food you planned to eat before you go to work, so do I. I don't have to go to the market just because you were lazy to go for yourself.'

See, he expressed that although it's only bread and he doesn't mind, there must be a limit after which it is violation of property. He did that without mentioning anything of the sort, and only by appealing to the human nature of the culprit. He asked them to put themselves in his shoes.

Based on this, take a second to ask yourself: 'what is there to gain from engaging in behaviour that doesn't lead to who I want to be?'. Answer truthfully before jumping to the next section.

REWARD

Powerlessness. That is the reward.

Powerlessness is the feeling we have when we believe that our actions have no impact, that they can't influence anything. It's the feeling that we are not to be taken seriously, and that our words are empty and invisible. All of that stems from a low self-esteem, from a lack of worth.

In my opinion, although a lack of worth can stem from many sources, it stems primarily from not knowing ourselves, from not understanding ourselves. Why? Because when we don't know *what* we want, and if we do, then *why* we want what we want, we end up doing what another tells us to do, not what we proposed to do (if we even proposed to do anything in the first place). We end up accepting what is happening to us without taking a stand. We end up believing the words of another in spite of the fact that our worth is giving to us by *ourselves* through our actions, not through the empty words of another! Does a lumberjack need constant and daily appreciation to be reminded or to know that their tree cutting skill is great? No!

You see, you can feel worthless as a result of always doing what another suggests. Not having a steady hand on the helm of your ship, and therefore *not being who you want to be* can lead to unworthiness. It's logical. If you always do what another tells you to do, you may start to subconsciously believe that what you want to do isn't right, that it isn't worth investing the energy, the stress, and the time. Otherwise why would you say 'yes' to their requests if you know that the behaviour you will adopt won't be *the kind of behaviour that leads to who you want to be*? How can you feel good about yourself if you let another dictate your life, *if you let another tell you who you want to be*?

But at a certain point you snap, and when that happens you become aggressive. You start yelling at people, you stop listening to what they have to say, you start trying to take control of those things which you have no control over, like their rights. You stop being civilised. Know that being aggressive is just shifting blame from the inability to defend yourself politely to the outer world for hurting you. It is this shifting of blame from the lack of understanding who you are (and the inability to stand by your choices because of fear) to the outer world because they 'dared' to hurt you! Realise now that the words of others have no power over us, for they are just that: words!

ANALYSE

Being passive is letting others decide for you. It's the belief that your actions and needs aren't important. It's the forfeit of your rights. Note that, just because you're passive, it doesn't mean people will necessarily respect you. On the contrary, it means that people will get to make choices for you, that they will abuse your kindness, that they will like you for the ability to be used according to their needs, and not for who you are. Where is the respect in that? Also, how can you *be who you want to be* if another makes choices for you?

Being aggressive is imposing orders instead of conversing. It's listening to reply, not to understand. It's the abuse of others' rights. It's trying to manipulate that which you have no control over. Remember that it isn't the thunder that helps the flower grow. Going back to the example from the *Illustrate* sub-section, we now find out that:

First I was passive and allowed my housemates to take bread because I thought it was a necessity, but it was a superfluity. They didn't take bread because they required one or two slices before they bought their own, they took bread because it was easier than buying their own. Because they were lazy thieves.

After, I became aggressive and I yelled at people, I even tried to shame them for this despicable behaviour. I told them to stop touching my stuff, but that fell on deaf ears. If I can't prove who it is, then the culprit can go on and do as he pleases.

Then I learned to become assertive. I understood that the problem won't be fixed by letting others step on me, and that it can't be fixed by yelling at them. And because it wasn't going to be fixed like that, that there is no point in wasting my time with stress since it doesn't change anything, or amount to anything. So I learned from my brother to give the opportunity for someone to take bread, but only if it is a necessity, and I informed them that if I see them abuse this second chance, that I will take it away. It worked for a while, and when it didn't, I started taking my things up to my room. We then caught the culprit because people started losing weight (nah, it's because all of a sudden someone had bread).

UNDERSTAND

See, *the purpose on which civilizations have been built is none other than reciprocity*. Think about all the times you had exchanges, be it if someone gave you something for free, or you gave someone something for free. Recall how both you and they always wanted to give something back, always wanted to balance the scale, to share the happiness. Whether it was a gift you gave or got, you and they always felt the compelling need to give something back to the other. We understood early in time that, if we have two bags of potatoes and someone else has two bags of meat, we can make one hell of a stew if we trade one bag in exchange for the other. This has stood the test of time as we have inter-continental shipments nowadays.

But what if the potato owner didn't share, but instead willingly gave their potato bag without expecting anything in return? Now that wouldn't be great, as it usually leads to oppression in the long-run. If someone demands something of us and we give it away willingly, chances are people will come back to demand more. Being comfortable is today's normal, and people abuse it like it's oxygen. Thus, we must make sure to detect these people before they make a nest in our kindness. Saying 'no' is quite easy as soon you know the difference between the terms 'benefactor' and 'manipulator'. This difference usually shows itself when a person gives us something, and when that happens we must look at it and think *'is this person a benefactor or a manipulator? **Is this person's intention pure or is this person about to manipulate me?'***

Remember that our entire human race is developed on the reciprocity function. A manipulator knows that the compelling desire to give something in return when you receive something is embedded in our behaviour, and abuses that if you allow it. Thus, you might see people who give you small favours and then ask for a big one, or who listen to you and then demand something, buy you a pizza and then asks your help. *Caveat Emptor* (Latin for 'buyer beware').

It is very important to be able to say 'no', be it either to someone or to yourself. I would like to think that, after reading this book and maybe occasionally coming back to it to revise some lessons, you now understand my point. The point that slowly but surely you are distancing yourself from your ego, and the way you're doing that is by questioning your behaviour with the *'but why?'* system. This allows you to get to know who you were when the ego was deciding your actions for you, and *who you want to be* now when deciding your actions for yourself. Deciding your actions based on answers is not enough for knowing your true self, and alike prudence, you must also stand by them and take responsibility.

Thus, I now ask you:

- How can you *be who you want to be* if you do not say 'no'? You must say 'no' because you know your limits, you know your preferences, and you know that the things you do not want to do go against your moral boundaries, against your wishes, against who you want to be.

- How can *doing something that you do not want to do* lead to *who you want to be*? (To not be confused with working in an industry, like sales, which thickens your skin because of rude and stupid customers, nobody likes that but it helps to build up a stronger future-you. I'm specifically talking about things like engaging in troublesome behaviour with your entourage).

OVERCOME

Saying 'no' gives you an empowered feeling, a sensation of being connected to your worth, of power over your choices. There are different scenarios in which we must make sure to say 'no', and all of them stem from the same place: listening to your soul, questioning if it goes against your moral boundaries and against *who you want to be*, and if it comes from a manipulator or a benefactor.

First of all, *we must categorise our actions in actions that <u>do lead</u> to who we want to be, and actions that <u>do not lead</u> to who we want to be.* We must understand where we stand in certain situations. For example, if we want to take care of our car and our brother drives recklessly, we must not give in to their request to give him the keys. Giving him the keys goes against *who you want to be*, which is a person that takes care of their car. You cannot drive for them, but you can prevent them from driving your car.

Second of all, *we must realise the difference between a manipulator and a benefactor.* We must look at the behaviour a person has and question ourselves if they have anything to gain from it. A manipulator usually does a small gesture (like buying us something to eat or drink, or bringing us something) to trigger the reciprocity law, and then asks for a favour. However, a benefactor gives us something without expecting and asking anything in return. Once we realise this difference, saying 'no' to a manipulator is easy because we realise that they are doing something for us only to win something in return. They are snakes, and alike Harry Potter, you can also speak to snakes, you just sometimes don't understand them immediately.

Third of all, *we must realise the difference between necessity or superfluity.* It is normal to step on your boundaries if it's about the true benefit of another soul, but not when it is not. Let's say that every time you take money out of your savings account there is a tax of 5%. There's no problem, in my opinion, with taking money out of your savings account when someone asks you to lend them money because they're poor and can't feed themselves. There is a problem with taking money out of your savings account when someone asks to buy something trivial, unnecessary, like a gaming console, a graphics card, or anything else superfluous. If they aren't in peril, or at death's door, you're not a douche. They're eager.

Lastly, *we need to question if the behaviour we're about to engage in leads to who we want to be.* The more you let your ego dissolve and get to know yourself, the more control and understanding of your boundaries you have. You now probably know what you want to do in most cases, why you support your choices in those cases, *and why you do not want to do the opposite in those situations.* If you know the reason *why you **do not** want to do some stuff,* and you go ahead and do it regardless, what do you have to gain from that? If you know that your action does not lead to *who you want to be,* why do it in the first place?

Now that we've defined the steps to understanding how to perceive assertiveness, let's go ahead and see what understanding this chapter will do for us:

Why should I be assertive? If I manage to be assertive, what will that realisation produce? What are the virtues that I will gain from being assertive? What is my mission?

I should be assertive in order to realise my true potential. I cannot fully be who I want to be if I always cross my moral boundaries and say 'yes' to everyone. If I declare that I do not want to partake in some sort of activity, and someone asks me again and again, I can refuse to engage.

If I manage to be assertive, the realisation produced will be that I am now even more in control. Life is like art, and art is a metaphor of control. You control the canvas, the tools, the colours, the subject, and nobody but yourself stands in your way, in its deepest and truest meaning. So too must you be assertive, must you declare your purpose, must you control your choices. You haven't just gotten out of your ego's control to just hand control back to some stranger, did you? Because that's what you're doing when you're not saying 'no'. You let someone else control you.

The virtues that I will gain from being assertive are justice, fortitude, and temperance.

My mission is to stand by my choices and support them. If I declare that I will study and better my life instead of partying every week and celebrating nothing, like my entourage does, then that is what I will do. I will not give in to instant gratification when the future looks so bright. I declared my choices, my wishes, my happiness, and doing opposite will bear no rewards. 'I haven't come this far to only come this far', as Ryan Serhant says. Consequently, I will now look at people's behaviour and understand whether they are a benefactor, or a manipulator. Even me with myself. Not only will I say 'no' to other people when they try to gain something, but I will also say 'no' to myself when I realise that I'm about to give in to behaviour that is not noble. Give in to behaviour that does not lead to *who I want to be,* so put the pizza on the ground and back away slowly! *police sirens in the background*

What to take away: It is important to know when to say 'no' because life is all about control. I hope you truly realise how damaging an ego's control over our life is, and how hard it has been (or is) to let go of it. Are you really willing to pass control over your life from one dictator to another, or are you ready to stand up for yourself and start living? The choice is yours.

Chapter 5
REALISE YOUR WORTH

The only feeling that can either put the world at your feet or you at the world's feet is self-confidence.
— ANDRA GEORGESCU

PURPOSE

The purpose of this chapter is to bring attention to the values you possess and those you *could* possess, and to attempt to make you understand that others' opinions of you does not reflect your real values. We will attempt to look at different ways of creating our worth.

INTROSPECTIVE

This chapter attempts to build on the previous ones by bringing to attention how we let ourselves assume that we're stupid if someone tells us that we're stupid, when that clearly isn't the case. We have moments when we make mistakes and, if you feel bad about yourself, then imagine what the person who damaged that 300 million dollars machine feels like. Now it shouldn't seem that bad that you spilled coffee on the floor, right? Good.

Now, we ask ourselves:

Why should I realise my worth? If I manage to realise my worth, what will that realisation produce? What are the virtues that I will gain from realising my worth? What is my mission?

DEFINE

What is *self-worth*? *Self-worth* is the feeling that we are good enough. It is the sensation that we are worthy to be accepted and loved as a fellow human being. Since acceptance and love is given by others (besides ourselves), we then say that *self-worth* is the feeling we get from proving to ourselves our abilities to be noble.

What are *expectations*? *Expectations* are imaginary beliefs regarding outcomes, based on the emotions we have at the given time, usually. When we ask our friends for help, we expect them to reply positive. When we didn't study as much as we should, we expect to fail the exam. When we help our friend, we expect them to help us in return when the time comes. When we want to impress someone, we expect to overachieve.

People grow up with different behaviours due to the bajillion possibilities of outer circumstances. For example, the kind person that has been betrayed will possibly grow up distrustful, unlike the kind person who was never been betrayed.

Thus, we will now attempt to find the common ground, the one where a kind person that was betrayed learns to *stop expecting the same from everyone*. We will also attempt to realise that *a mistake is only a blink in our existence,* and that *we are the sum of our achievements, not of our mistakes.*

ILLUSTRATE

I rented a house with a bunch of friends of mine. I had a job where I worked the afternoons, so for me it was ok to stay up late. However, a friend of mine had a morning job, so going to bed early was supposedly the only logical course of action. He decided to stay up late one night.

The following morning I had to drop the kids off at the pool, but he was in the bathroom, using it to wash his shoes in the sink in a hurry state because he had to go to work in 30 minutes. To make things worse, he didn't have anything to eat, was having a bad mood, and was probably going to be late. I politely informed him that, for his own health, he needed to evacuate the bathroom as soon as possible. He told me to have a go at it...

Thus ensues a ten minutes argument about how I find it weird that he wants me to have bowel movements with him in the bathroom, standing next to me whilst washing his shoes, and how he finds it weird that I'm the 'only friend that has this problem'. Five minutes into the fight and I tell him to see a therapist, to which he replied that he's spoken to his therapist and was notified that he doesn't need me in his life anymore. He doesn't have a therapist but thanks, message received.

Based on this, take a second to ask yourself: 'what is there to gain from taking another's opinion to heart?'. Answer truthfully before jumping to the next section.

REWARD

Worthlessness. That is the reward we get when we get hurt by someone close to us. It doesn't matter the circumstance, it doesn't matter if we were right or wrong. The only thing that matters is that it hurts, and even more importantly, that you can learn from it if you pay attention.

Worthlessness is the feeling of emptiness. It's the feeling of keeping your head down, chin-to-chest. It's the feeling that all of your achievements are worth absolutely nothing, when that isn't the truth. Worthlessness is a result of being overwhelmed by emotions.

But I like to tell myself that that's about it. As emotions are temporary states brought on by neurophysiological changes, if you make sure to not overthink you will regain the emotional balance sooner or later. Soon you will realise that the sum of achievements from your life didn't just up-and-vanished. You still are your greatest feats, and you will pass this moment too, and consequently, supposedly, and hopefully learn from it.

ANALYSE

Most of the times the problem is not the problem, the problem is the attitude about the problem. The aforementioned friend decided to sacrifice his time in order to gain some temporary happiness by gaming, but in doing so he sacrificed both his mood and mine in the process.

The expected outcome of that night was identical to a monthly paycheque: you save money and then you spend what's left, not the other way around. But instead, he went to bed late and tired, woke up tired and moody, didn't have time to practice a normal morning routine, had the pressure of time not being on his side, and thus he let out his anger on the people around him. This is my best friend since high school, and his words struck me deeply, but I am forever grateful to that moment. Love you bro.

UNDERSTAND

Now, we must look at this from the analytical way. Was there anything that could've been done? Yes and no. There is a line that we should not cross, as beyond it lies the inhuman part: should we expect people to not treat us as we treat them? But if we end up thinking that we shouldn't expect the same from our best friend then what's the point in having a best friend? On the other hand, we end up hurt in the process if we continue to expect the same from people. What is the correct way? Is there a correct way?

About others: Yes there is, and weirdly enough it requires you to *not expect the same from everyone,* your best friend included, but not in the way you might think, and definitely not the inhuman way.

I think that the best solution to stop suffering in this case is to realise your worth. I asked myself 'if today I'd get the same insult from him, would I feel hurt?', and the answer was no. When I pursued this with an eight-year-old's logic of hierarchical understanding using the *'but why?'* system, I realised that it's because I can't control people. I cannot control their anger, their opinions, their actions. On top of that, I realised that *their opinion of me is not my true value.* 'Worry about your character, not your reputation. Your character is who you are, and your reputation is who people think you are', says John Wooden.

Know that we cannot be the hero in everyone's story, and regardless of how good we are, we can never please everyone, and we shouldn't for that matter. We should be good to others and respect them (justice), but we must first be good to ourselves in order to do that (prudence). Thus, the best thing we can do is to realise that another's opinion of us doesn't represent our true value since *we're the ones who know* what's good for us, not them. Based on this, we realise that their opinion is not our true value, but *only **the value they believe us to have** in that exact moment due to their current perception!*

How many times have people insulted us and we let it get to us? Did them calling us stupid meant that we are stupid? No! How many times did people laugh at our dreams? Did them calling our dreams weak meant that our dreams were weak? No! I wouldn't be the great artist I consider myself to be without the help of those who supported me, and without ignoring the rude ones who tried to bring me down for whatever reason.

We can always be better, for I am now a better artist than I was 10 years ago, so their opinion of me 10 years ago, in that exact moment and circumstance, is only a perception of my then-current skill. But since I can be better, I proved it slowly and surely over the course of 10 years. Not with words, but with actions! And if you remember the *Prologue* chapter, then you remember that I told you how an opinion is made from what you feel, see, and hear. So if another's opinion is made of what they think, feel, see, and hear, then isn't that the processed information from their sense? Isn't that perception? Isn't that perspective? Isn't that only one face of the situation? It is.

Now imagine if I allowed their opinions of me to stop me, and I didn't believe in myself. I wouldn't be today the proud (respectfully) and happy person that I am with my art. Thus, when someone is rude to us, their opinion is a reflection of themselves, not of us. I'm not saying that they are telling a lie and you shouldn't listen to it, for my art wasn't great back then. I'm saying that you should be assertive and listen to understand, see if there's anything you can learn, look at it as a challenge, not as rude, and move on. You got something to gain from a challenge.

About ourselves: I now want to direct your attention to the people who lie. People who lie, for a while, get what they desire if they are successful in lying. It isn't a wonderful life to live, and surely you remember when you lied in order to get an extra cookie or some instant gratification (see chapter *Addiction*). It felt good for a while, and then it didn't. And if you did continue down this path, you realised eventually how bad it felt not only because if everyone found out about your lies they would stop trusting you, but also because of the struggle to keep all the lies in check.

It's easy to summon a memory and to describe it once or as many times as needed, but it's hard to remember the exact words you used when you lied, and that's why lies catch up to us eventually. Now why do I mention this? I mention this because I hope that by using the law of contrast you will now regard exponentially better the nobility of an act.

Nobility is the trait of having and showing admirable qualities, and it can be created through a snowball effect. It is the continuous improvement of self through minor daily incrementations, or weekly incrementations. Remember the chapter *The Room*? If you want to feel worthy, start by looking at your immediate surrounding for things that are not in order. It can either be to make your bed, to wash your dishes, to hoover your room. *L1.* If those are already completed, take an imaginary step outside of that intensity level and focus on the things that need fixing in the next area, *L2.* It took me a long time to understand that the more I am engaged in the present moment and the more I do the task now instead of leaving it for later when I'm tired and less willing to do, the better my self-worth and my general day is. Discipline is key.

Give it a try for a day and see how you feel. See how entering your apartment and seeing your bed made, no dishes to be cleaned, and the floor hoovered makes you feel like you're worth a million bucks!

OVERCOME

As with everything in life, there is usually a good side and a bad side, and the good side of watching content creators (YouTube, Twitch, etc.) is that we can observe one thing: that, although we have a feeling that we know them, we do not know them.

Christian Poulos, an influencer that I respect says that 'social media is a highlight reel, not reality'. Think about it: everyone tries to look good in front of camera and to publish content that reflects their best behaviour and best features, otherwise the video won't have traction and they won't increase their chance of getting subscribers, revenue, etc. What we don't see in those videos, however, is their bad side, and we shouldn't for the matter. We are watching them for inspiration, or because they are funny, or to learn something, but we have no actual idea about what their life is like since we haven't walked a mile in their shoes. We have no idea about their daily struggles, their insecurities, etc.

I now want to reverse and reflect that back on you. People see the version of *you* that dresses nicely, is polite, tries to smile, and does its best. They have no idea if you have any sort of pain, be it either physical or emotional, they have no idea if you have enough money to eat today, if you're a student at a prestige university, and other struggles or amazing traits you have. They just see a human and they judge on what they see, and *what they see is not what it actually is! Not only do people not check if their thoughts and facts are perception-based or reality-based before they release them, but you are not who you are in a moment, but who you are in your entirety!*

We all have weak moments, and sometimes people catch a glimpse of that and shamelessly point it out, sometimes in a rude manner. You are not your mistake, for that is only a blink in your entire existence. Instead you are your entire existence itself! What they saw is not what it is, but they have no shame to realise that they should get the bigger picture before they speak, so let them. Remember the barking dog and the magic spell? Yeah.

'Great, so how do I realise and increase my worth?', you ask.

First of all, **you must realise that achievements bring us worthiness.** We have a self-evaluation mechanism behind our eyes, and that is focused on our ability to prove ourselves, be it to us or to others. Why are you happy when you aced a test? Why are you happy when everyone likes the food you cooked? Why are you happy when people laugh at your jokes? It's because you achieved something. You realised something. *You've proved to yourself the amazing qualities and power you have.* When you go to bed after a day like that, you will feel proud, worthy, and will be smiling ear to ear.

Second of all, **you must realise that without achievements you can't feel worthy.** I'm not saying that as a retired CEO you will feel worthless. I'm saying that you have to get to be a CEO in the first place.

I'm not saying that you have to show the world on social media how you bought clothes to a homeless person, I'm saying you should give what you can to a homeless person, preferably anonymously. Whatever you do, you have a power and a choice to express that power, and if you choose to do good, you will feel good. I do not know the reason why, but I imagine it's because other's appreciation allows us to feel something we can't feel from our own appreciation. I mean, it feels good when another is smiling with their eyes and from their heart, and their burden lifted as a result of your help, doesn't it?

Third of all, *you must realise that you are not a temporary mistake, but the sum of achievements.* You are human, and erring is natural. The problem appears when you expect to act perfect towards something/someone in order to impress, and upon failing, you feel bad all day. The problem appears when you believe another's laughter about your dream or mistake is the highest value your dream or existence represents. People laugh, and they're allowed to, *so be realistic and check if there is truth to what they say*. If so, accept the truth, learn what you can, move on, and rinse and repeat.

Lastly, *you must realise that you must not be a slave to achievements.* Process and progress are important, as you will see in section 3, chapter 2: *Happiness is the journey, not the destination.* What I say in this chapter is not 'walk around arrogantly proud of your achievements', but 'don't feel down for a temporary mistake, instead learn from it and realise that your past achievements are still there, and you aren't the temporary mistake pointed out by someone!'.

With every lesson our worth grows, so let's look at the introspective questions and answer them:

Why should I realise my worth? If I manage to realise my worth, what will that realisation produce? What are the virtues that I will gain from realising my worth? What is my mission?

I should realise my worth in order to realise my worth. Keep it simple. Nobody can realise your worth but yourself. Only you and your actions of accepting who you are, accepting who you want to be, *accepting your flaws, and working on those you can correct can give you a sense of self-worth (process and progress)*. Positive actions lead to positive thoughts, so start by looking at your immediate surrounding.

Is your bed made? Are your dishes washed? Are your clothes folded and placed in their respective place? This is only a preparatory step, a façade to prepare you for the real life. It's a façade that is made to get you into the mindset of questioning the state of your environment (which is a result of your choices), and into the mindset of bettering yourself objectively. Small victories lead to lesser regrets. Who do you think feels more worthy? Someone who is appreciated for having a tidy room with one or two things that can be improved, or someone who is scolded for not making their bed, for not tidying their clothes, for not putting things back in their respective places, for not hoovering and mopping their bedroom, etc.?

If I manage to realise my worth, the realisation produced by that will be an unshakable power. You will know what you like and what you dislike, and you will be stronger in making decisions and standing by them. The words of others won't shake you and make you doubt anymore, and that is because you know what you believe in, you researched what you believe in (and updated or discarded the outdated information), and you stand by what you believe in. Consequently, others' words won't shake you because you will now understand that they can only judge you on surface-level behaviour, and that they have no idea what is going on behind curtains. *Their reflection is based on a moment in time where you seemed weak, not on your entire lifespan!*

The virtues that I will gain from realising my worth are prudence, justice, fortitude, and temperance. Nice combo!

My mission is to realise that it is easier for people to point out others' mistakes than it is to acknowledge their own short-comings. But what does it mean to point out mistakes, if not the lack of attention to oneself? Are their beds made? Are their dishes clean? No, they're probably not, but yours probably are, and because you are the sum of your achievements, you are not worthless.

What to take away: When someone who actually cares about you notices that you did a mistake, they usually ask you to sit down, to go through the process that got you to do the mistake, they listen to you, understand your point, raise questions if they didn't understand something, and then make a conclusion to which you reply with 'yes, that's what I meant', or 'no, let me clear that up'. Anyone else is just a drop in the ocean that you won't remember in the future, so don't now.

FOREGONE

Chapter 6
DON'T EXPLAIN YOURSELF

Never explain yourself. Your friends don't need it and your enemies won't believe it.
— ZIAD K. ABDELNOUR

PURPOSE

The purpose of this chapter continues the discussion of self-worth, and illustrates how explaining ourselves damages our self-worth when used in the wrong situation.

INTROSPECTIVE

Continuing on the topic of worth, we must now question what explanations are, who are the judges, who we give our power to, why would we do that, and what would be the benefits of doing that. For example, what happens when we fall and someone tries to insult us at our weakest point? Do we explain ourselves, do we not, and if we do: *why do we decide to do it*?

We will discuss this after looking at this chapter's exercises and asking ourselves:

Why should I not explain myself? If I manage to stop explaining myself, what will that realisation produce? What are the virtues that I will gain from not explaining myself? What is my mission?

FOREGONE

DEFINE

What are *explanations*? *Explanations* are both a statement that attempts to make something clear, and a justification for an action performed. It is an educated analysis of where you went wrong and how you could do better.

When and *why* are explanations important? Explanations are important when justifying a situation. Usually an inconvenience is what triggers an explanation, be it a work inconvenience or a general life inconvenience, and explaining yourself works as both an answer for the party, and also as an answer for yourself.

ILLUSTRATE

As I was growing up *I had no idea of privacy*, and I hope that you can relate when I say that I used to believe that other people are just like me, so if I'm kind then they surely must be kind too. That is not the case, unfortunately. I am a very honest person and I used to answer everything without thinking twice. There was no reason to not say the truth when someone asked me something, but I always felt weird when all the relatives asked me questions about the problems I have at home (nosy little miscreants, taking advantage of a child). As I grew up and got to the dating point, I once had a girlfriend who had a lot of money. I sometimes asked her for a loan since she had a savings account, and asked her to wait until I got my salary. Now this was all nice and dandy but we got to a point where I asked and she refused to lend me. I asked her 'why?' and she said that she doesn't have to explain herself to me, and that I can do an effort and wait till the end of the month.

Based on this, take a second to ask yourself: 'what is there to gain from explaining myself?'. Answer truthfully before jumping to the next section.

REWARD

Homelessness. That is the reward. What do I mean by that?

What I mean is that you invite in your life (your home) all those who you engage with, and if you make the mistake of giving your power away instead of keeping it to yourself by not explaining your reasons behind what you do, soon you will realise that when they leave (as soon as they finished giving you their two cents regarding their fears and insecurities about the plan/goal you have, and how it's wrong and you shouldn't), you will be powerless.

What I mean by homeless is powerless, deenergized, doubtful. We have a limited amount of power every day, and depending on our nervous system, a limited control over our power. Now, if we get angry, moody, sad, confrontational, or whatever else is not noble, we are giving away our power. It takes energy to engage, and once you are done and you move on, some of your power went away. Think about how you feel after a confrontation, how you feel after you explain yourself although you know you shouldn't. You punch yourself afterwards, and question the reason why you did that, in spite of your gut feeling saying no. Do this with five people every day, and you'll be left tired, crying, feeling down, etc.

You're left homeless when you realise that you had no reason to try to change someone's mind, or to try to explain why what you're doing (gymnastics, art, science, etc.) is good. The moment you start to feel homeless is when the people you explained yourself to get up and leave. People are curious, and soon another will come to take its place and tell you how your dream is wrong, based on their fear and insecurities.

My mother taught me this saying, and I finally understand it: 'people judge according to their own acts'. Look at Chris Hemsworth and Tom Hiddleston: there were newspapers where they were referred to as 'no-names' when they joined Marvel for the Thor franchise. But who has the last laugh now? Those who didn't explain themselves, but instead proved themselves!

I'm not saying that what you want to do is good or that it will work, I'm saying that you have to give it a try if it is morally right and respects the rights of others. Think about drawing: I would have never reached the point of making great art, being proud, and feeling worthy if I listened to others who told me that I'm not good 10 years ago, and that I'll never be good. I have tried to explain to them that I will be good, and you know what they did? They countered that with another reason from their logic, like how I'll never earn money from art, or how nobody appreciates art anymore, or whatever their own fear about art is. People are comfortable, and they believe to have time, and that is why they prefer to do a 9-to-5 job than to take a risk, so no matter what you'll tell them, they'll always have an excuse/response to counter your argument with, and that's because they don't have the courage you have, and can only see fear as a consequence. Thus my mother's saying stands the test of time.

ANALYSE

I was young and stupid and *expected* that, just because I have the apartment and she lives with me, she also has to do something for me, sort of a *Quid Pro Quo* (Latin for 'exchange of services'). You know when someone asks you for something every month and you get to a point where you have to teach that person to self-sustain? It was an identical situation to the 'give a man a fish' story. It's not that she didn't want to give me money, it was that she had to find a way to teach me to be self-sustaining, and because I have always been good at finding solutions, she had to restrict my access to the reason of her choice in order to make me realise that there is something called privacy, and that she is allowed to have it.

UNDERSTAND

Her and I had an amazing relation, matching humour levels, we helped one another however we could, she is not the villain in the story is what I'm trying to say in case my writing butchered her actual character. I was. Remember that you have surface-level information and that, although it might seem like an easy task to lend money and something you might do without thinking if you were in her situation, it does actually get tiring, as I went through it recently and it drained me.

Now about her motive, I am very good at finding solutions and being a positive person. She probably thought that if she tells me a reason as to why she can't lend me money, I'd find a solution and the loop would go on and on, so she had to do what she had to do, and I thank her even today for that good lesson. As I mentioned, explanations are used to make something clear or to justify an action, thus they are not a mandatory behaviour.

In this case she was right to not explain herself because first of all her purpose was to teach me a lesson, and most people usually learn best when they come to a realisation themselves. Second of all, she doesn't need to explain to me why she doesn't want to do something. That's her choice, she knows why she chose to do that, and she doesn't have to explain it to me. I am not a judge, I am not God, I am not her mother, I was but her partner. *What right do I have to ask her for her reason?*

Another situation where you don't have to explain yourself is when the explanation falls on deaf ears. Imagine this: you have back pain every morning, your relationship is close to ending, your pet died, and still you manage to wake up and to do your chores, you are a student at a prestige university, you go to work with a smile on your face, and you keep it all to yourself since nothing changes if you mention problems you can't control, so why bother? You do this every day, but one day on your way home you're tired and you try to take your phone out but accidently drop your coffee. Opposite of the road is a group of teenagers that starts laughing at you. If you drop your coffee because you're tired from working six days per week, have a broken relationship home, and your pet died, nobody will know. They will laugh because they noticed a random person dropped a random item, something that is funny for teenagers. And that is okay:

- The first thing to understand is that you don't have to explain yourself to them because it will fall on deaf ears. They don't care about their problems, and even if they do, *why should they care about yours?* If you explain yourself to them they'll process the information, discard it because it has no value and therefore no impact on their lives, and move on.
- The second thing to understand is that explaining yourself to them won't solve your issue. You'll still be tired, your coffee is still spilled, your life is still troubled. You win nothing by sharing, however, you win by understanding that you can't control what happened. You can laugh with them, or be sad at them, but not both.

Based on these two steps, you now need to understand that although this example was probably exaggerated, and definitely imaginary, the same idea applies to your personal life. How many times did you try to explain yourself to someone, only to realise that not only did it go through one ear and out the other, but you also felt disappointed because you thought they cared and because you wasted your time explaining yourself? How many times did explaining yourself to the wrong person solved the problem? How many times did the universe align in such a way to make your life miserable, and no matter how hard you pushed, it just didn't work out for you? Some people don't care about understanding others' issues, others care only to gain, others only seem to care but actually manipulate, so be careful who you explain yourself to and how much you say when you explain yourself.

OVERCOME

Let's look at everything so far. If explanations are used to justify action, and someone asks something of us that we don't need to justify because it is none of their business, we can refuse to explain ourselves. It's like when the police asks questions and the lawyer responds by saying 'there's no need to answer that'. They are just nosy. Some because that's their nature, others because they are keen on telling you what the right way is and how you're wrong.

However, there are some good people out there who actually care for you and who will try to guide you correctly and without any benefit to them if you let them. Thus, your duty is to find out with time who is trying to live your life, and who is trying to help you. Who is trying to give you orders, and who is trying to help you. Who is being nosy, and who is being genuinely interested in your own advantage.

Don't be afraid to ask a person *'why are you asking me this?'*, or *'what do you hope to understand if I answer your question?'* if you feel like the question pertains to your private life and has nothing to do with the topic of the discussion. Alike the *Be assertive* chapter, you need to realise if they are benefactors or manipulators, so use the above two questions and listen to their actual answer, the one behind their words.

'That's great, but how do we do this?', you ask.

First of all, *you must realise that there must be a reason to explain yourself, otherwise there's no reason to explain yourself.*

Unless in court, I don't think anyone has the right to judge your choices, as long as they (your choices) are morally right. That doesn't mean that they won't judge you, it just means that they shouldn't. You have one life, and you can live is as you wish to, so pursue whatever you desire, and let not the fear of small minds stop you. You already know that only your decision to think of their words as offensive instead of challenging would be the only obstacle in your way.

Second of all, *you must question the questioner what they hope to achieve by understanding your answer.* If you know yourself to be in the right and without mistake, you must still question them and understand that maybe they see something you don't from your perspective. Thus, listen to their answer and see if they are a benefactor, or a manipulator. If they are nosy, or genuinely helpful. There is always something to learn from listening, be it that you need to move on, or to take something into consideration.

Third of all, *you can choose to explain yourself once, and then tell them to back off if they are manipulators.* Just as you can leave from a table, so too can you leave from a conversation. If you see that the conversation is heading towards the generic 'but you'll never make it because X and Y', you must tell them that you have done your part and listened to them out of courtesy. If they have nothing to add besides their fears, then it's better to not say anything at all.

Now let's look at the introspective questions and to answer them:

Why should I not explain myself? If I manage to stop explaining myself, what will that realisation produce? What are the virtues that I will gain from not explaining myself? What is my mission?

I should not explain myself because I know my worth, and therefore I know what I like and what I don't, and I don't need to give people an understanding of that. If you choose something and someone questions your choice with that air of putrid invasiveness, you do not need to explain yourself. You can actually reverse it and ask 'why should I not?', and see their point of view, weight it against your own and see if there is something you can learn from it. A small note I'd like to add is that knowing what you like and don't is something that takes years of discovering *and understanding*, so make sure to not come off as ignorant and rude. In fewer words: don't be rude but don't accept rude people either, listen to their point, take what is valuable, say thank you, and move on.

If I manage to stop explaining myself, the realisation produced is that I am even more in control of my actions and my choices, and I fortify my presence by standing by the choices I make. There is nothing more powerful than someone who believes in themselves (as long as it is morally right), and how can you demonstrate that you believe in yourself if you keep explaining your actions to everyone. Work in silence, focus on your goal, understand your motives, and push forward. The more people know about why you do stuff, the more they try to bring you down, and that is because a great idea can't be understood by a small mind! Inside a small mind roams fear and doubt constantly because they're afraid of knowing who they *truly* are as a consequence of letting their ego drive their lives! As a consequence of not being noble, of not being prudent! Those who have nothing interesting in their lives talk about others, remember this! That is why people ask for explanations for your actions, so they can judge you against their logic, the logic driven by their ego that, as stated in the *Question your actions* chapter, doesn't want to change. They can't even fathom the work you put in, the goals you have, the dreams you dream, and they never will if they don't change their logic! That is why you don't explain yourself!

The virtues that I will gain from not explaining myself are prudence, fortitude, and temperance.

My mission is to ascertain whether someone is asking me something to teach me or to be nosy, and if it's their business to do so. Whether someone is a benefactor or a manipulator. If *explanations* are both a statement that attempts to make something clear, and a justification for an action performed, and that person is clearly asking me to bring me down and to laugh at me with his little mind, then I am better off on my way. No need to waste my breath.

Quis Custodiet Ipsos Custodes (Latin for 'who will guard the guards themselves?'). Who do you decide is judge in your life?

What to take away: People cheer on you when you're a baby and try to bring you down when you're an adult. If you look at someone and won't take advice from them, then please don't take critique either.

Chapter 7
GUILT & GRATITUDE

Do not indulge in dreams of having what you have not, but reckon up the chief of the blessings you do possess, and then thankfully remember how you would crave for them if they were not yours.
— MARCUS AURELIUS

PURPOSE

The purpose of this chapter is to make us take a step back and to look at the bigger picture, at the gifts that we possess, and at the state our life would be in without them. How much guilt do people who had it all and lost it feel, and how hard life humbles them into being grateful afterwards.

INTROSPECTIVE

Anything past sustenance is a fad, an intense and short-lived hype, a craze. I've had both state-of-the-art technology and cheap technology too, I've lived in houses my parents own that are worth half a million pounds, and in studio flats worth 20,000 pounds, I've dined at big restaurants in London where a stake was £300, and I've also ate a £3 kebab. These experiences all eventually led to one thing: the philosophical school of Stoicism.

We all want a new apartment, a new car, and the latest technology, and there's nothing wrong with that. The problem appears when we take for granted the things we have, instead of appreciating them. We have to look at them and appreciate how miserable we would be without them, and how we would crave for them back if we were to lose them. Ultimately, the old saying 'money doesn't bring happiness' is a universal truth because money brings comfort, not *true* happiness. For now, let's turn our attention to our exercises:

Why should I practice gratitude? If I manage to practice gratitude, what will that realisation produce? What are the virtues that I will gain from practicing gratitude? What is my mission?

DEFINE

What is *gratitude*? *Gratitude* is the act of acknowledging and appreciating. It is the respect we show life for the numerous gifts that it gave us, starting with health and ending with material things. It's the honour we show our life for how far it has taken us.

What is *guilt*? *Guilt* is the sensation we feel when we have remorse. When we regret having done something, or *not* having done something. *Guilt* for me, however, has a secondary, subtler meaning: hope.

At any point we can be hit by misfortune and humbled into a sorry state. We never truly appreciate what we have until we lose it, and afterwards we miss our past-selves and how well life was going for us. Regardless of the state we find ourselves in, we should always find time to be grateful for all the good memories we made, and if not, then for the potential we have to make better memories once we decide to change our life. There is literally nothing to be found in ungratefulness, but everything in gratefulness.

ILLUSTRATE

I had an example about my country, about how I earned €208 per month for two years, and how once I moved to London I started making in one month what I made in six months back in my home country. Although a good example, it was too obvious, so I scrapped that.

Something happened today that I feel like it's a better example. A subtler one, at least. Remember how we said that 'we should question everything because *things are not always what they seem to be*'? Based on that, here's today's illustration.

I live in a studio flat that could be better. There is only one source of heating: the air conditioning in the main room. The only taps that have hot water are the shower and the bathroom sink. The kitchen tap has water that reflects the outside weather, so it's always really cold in winter.

It's the end of January and it's snowing. I am washing dishes today and complaining about how we're already in 2022, and how it's a darn shame that there is no heater in the bathroom, that there is no hot water in the kitchen sink, that there are no heaters anywhere, and that my hands and feet are freezing. As I'm washing dishes on autopilot, my mind is at my book, revisiting chapters, ideas, seeing what can be improved and what should be replaced. The latest chapter I'm currently working on is this exact one, *Guilt & Gratitude*, and although I am the author of the book and the keeper of my lessons, I many times lose track of them too. The benefit gained from years of experience is that I wake up faster or even catch myself before I breach my own laws.

As I'm going through all the things I mention in this chapter, I question myself if there is anything I can apply today because the water is really cold, and I'm starting to go down the 'man, blast this place, I can't wait to move' alley.

Based on this, take a second to ask yourself: 'what is there to gain from being ungrateful?'. Answer truthfully before jumping to the next section.

REWARD

Negative bias. That is the reward. Negative bias is the tendency to only focus on the negative. It is the absence of colour. It is the focus on one's toes.

We've all been sad, mad, moody, disgruntled. Maybe even traumatized by the past, with the inability to get past it. That is a possible result of ungratefulness. Some people, like me, have had a long time of fighting their past, sometimes winning, other times doing more research. It is not a nice place to be in, and it sucks you of power, appetite, and life. But, as Carl Jung puts it, 'I am not what happened to me, I am what I choose to become'.

The thing we can do to get over it is to stop looking at our toes and to bring some colour in our life by remembering to be grateful for what we have, and among other important things like the ability to make our life better with our choices, by focusing on our health. By being grateful for our health, for the chance and privilege to wake up another day, to push through the challenges of today, to learn, and to better ourselves. By realising that the past is the past and we cannot change it, but that we can learn from it. The past has no power over the present, we give it power over the present.

ANALYSE

Just as you stop at a gas station and you quickly use the restroom without looking up to check for spiders, so too should you proceed in life. If you are afraid of spiders and go in the restroom looking for them, you're going to find them and you're never going to do what you proposed on doing. However, if you go in knowing that there is a risk, but decide to only focus on the things you can control, you will get in and out with the task done and minimum damage. It is very easy to get caught up in your life and to focus on the problems that appear and pile up, to go searching for problems and only focus on them, and that is what I was doing. I looked at my problems not with the intent to solve them, but with the intent to cry about them. I was sad and tired and all I wanted was for them to miraculously vanish.

Over the past few years I practiced gratitude not only in what I have, but also in what I didn't. As I was washing dishes today and crying about my freezing hands, I thought about my great-grandparents, and how they had -20°C or -30°C every winter, and how their winter wasn't what our winter is today with climate change. They had winter from December until February, heavily snowing every day. Upon realising that, I became grateful for not having -30°C winter for three months, for not having -30°C in general, and for not having as much winter as they did.

With that realisation came the following idea: just because they did it doesn't mean I have to; we live in 2022 and I can easily find a better place. But since they've done it, *I can do it too.* So my point wasn't that *because people suffered, I should suffer too*, but instead it was that *if those people suffered and survived, I can suffer and survive too!* You can go ahead and laugh (because I am laughing) about how I'm comparing -20°C or -30°C to washing dishes for 5 minutes with cold water, but this is what got me through, and if it looks stupid but it works, it isn't stupid.

No reason to focus on what I can't control. I just have to be grateful it isn't something serious and that winter will soon be over, and I'll be able to move to a better place. To top things off, I called my mom to see how she is, and such. She told me that the power went out and has been out since yesterday, that she is cold, that she doesn't have cooked food and warm water, and that she has to hang up because she has little battery and is saving it for emergency messages. Imagine how bad I felt about myself when I slept with the air conditioning on, when I washed my dishes, and when I cooked my food, and complained about all of that afterwards.

UNDERSTAND

We know that there are rewards in good behaviour, but what about *bad* behaviour? Usually when we fight with someone, we fight because we care. If the person is prior to dissolving their ego, the person fights because they want to protect themselves. If the person is subsequent to dissolving their ego, the person fights because they want to make things right. Hate, wars, and fights are born from different reasons:

- Love (protection)
- Envy & jealousy (insecurity)
- Ego (misunderstanding)

So we can agree that there is usually some sort of reward that we have in mind whenever we act, regardless of it coming from good or bad behaviour. Afterall, the balance between *the effort we make* and *the reward we get* must always be inclined down towards the former, for nobody wants to work hard and receive almost nothing. But what if I told you that, in my humble opinion, there is a reward if you shift the way you look at the world? What if I told you that guilt is the reward of ungratefulness (besides negative bias), and by my own extension, hope?

Remember that in the *define* sub-section, when defining *guilt*, I said that it has a secondary meaning for me: hope. What I meant by that is that when we feel guilty, we feel so because we have hope that we *are* better than this. We have the guilt that makes us think of the numerous choices that got us in that situation, and consequently hope, because we know that we are better than this (prior to dissolving the ego we think that we are better in an arrogant way, like the world owes us something when in reality nobody owes us anything). We find ourselves in a position where we follow the hierarchical thread of mistakes and reach the culprit, the choice that made us go down this path, and we scold ourselves afterwards. We scold ourselves because we realise the error in our judgement, and compliment it by being astonished that we would ever do such an error. That we would ever act this way.

I keep mentioning *prior and subsequent to dissolving the ego* and, honestly, I don't think it matters if you're arrogant when *thinking* (emphasis on the word *thinking*, not publicly exclaiming) that you are better than a situation. I think it's okay to pass through life with the idea that you are better than something or someone (in a competitive and sportsmanship way, obviously), be it driven by ego or by your true self. Usually we humble ourselves by putting to test our preconceived ideas, and end up either being proven wrong by the harsh reality, which leads to learning more about your current self, or confirm it by actually wining and proving that we are indeed better. Both lead to understanding oneself. As Mike Mentzer puts it, 'potential was only the expression of a possibility. Something that could be assessed accurately only in retrospect'.

It would only be a problem when you shame someone, and when you don't realise your limits. When you would do the horrendous mistake of pointing out something about someone that can't be changed in five minutes or less, or at all, like genetics. Be grateful that you are healthy and beautiful, think to yourself that you are healthier and prettier than some (and uglier than other), be just and honest, and most importantly, remember that looks will pass, and the only thing you should actively pursue is ever-lasting knowledge. We have general ideas of what great minds used to look (Socrates, Plato, Chrysippus, Marcus Aurelius, Epictetus, Seneca), but we don't know for sure what they truly looked like. What we know for sure is their knowledge, their written lessons that transcend time itself and are available today.

Humble yourself. Let go of your pride. You didn't work for your genetics, you have no control over them, so stop feeling like you achieved something. You want to feel proud? Do good! Realise how easy it is to be evil, to open your mouth and ruin someone's day. Take choices that change your life, which make you better than you were yesterday! Be grateful for what you have, but remember that *the only thing in your control is your mind.* Not your body organs, not your genetics, not the people around, not your mother and father. Since the only thing you can control is your mind, then the only thing you should and will be *truly* (emphasis on *truly*) proud of when the day is over and you get in bed is your personal achievements. Those that you created with your choices, not those you have from choices outside of your control (how pretty you are, how tall you are, etc).

OVERCOME

DON'T TAKE THINGS FOR GRANTED! Remember that life is not made of titanium, and that everything can break. That works in two ways, both in our favour if we're smart:

First of all, *you should realise that all the items in your possession are destructible,* and should detach yourself from those which form the illusion of necessity, those without which you think life wouldn't be the same. They are, after all, replaceable, be that your phone, your laptop, your furniture, your car, and what else.

Second of all, *remember to be grateful for them, nevertheless.* Just because you would be just as happy without them doesn't mean they don't make your life easier. How miserable would life be without a smartphone, a laptop, a job? You don't need shoes to run, but they bloody help.

I was looking at random youtubers that gave advice on how to be happier and I came across one that resonated with me. He said that there is an easy way to get happier, and that is to grab a pen and paper and focus on the things that you are grateful for. Imagine a bottle that is laying down on a platform, and this bottle is half full and marked at the middle. If you tilt it to the left side and leave it like that, the liquid will stay there. But if you tilt it to the right side and leave it like that, the liquid will move and stay on the right side now. The ability to tilt the bottle is in your hands.

If you focus on the problems you have and stay there, nothing good can come out of it. Anxiety and sadness will be the constant in your life. But when you decide to take a step back, to think about the bigger picture, to think about your life and all the good things in your life, be it either that you recently moved with your mates or that you're moving to your house, or about your new job or your new promotion, or about your independence or soon-to-come independence, or about your health and the health of your parents, life gets better. Too many times we take for granted our health and that of our loved ones, too many times we take for granted the roof over our heads, the food from our fridge, the mates from our life. Too many times we despair about problems that come and go, and let them control us. This has got to stop.

I understand that life beats us down sometimes, but I also understand that *we stay there as long as we let ourselves to stay there*. We can get in our bed, close our curtains, browse Reddit, and distract ourselves from the ugliness that our 'life' got us in, or we can get up and realise that we can do something about it. Instead of wasting time and distracting ourselves from the truth we can instead face it, charge ourselves with power (by being grateful), and then hit it head-on. The steps to start being grateful are as follows:

- The first step is to grab a pen and paper.
- The second step is to remove all distractions around you, to close your eyes, to ask yourself with your mind-voice 'What am I grateful for?', and to answer truthfully.
- The third step is to write down 'I am grateful for' and to write the first thing that comes to your mind. Don't even think about it, just let it write itself on paper. Then write again 'I am grateful for' and write whatever comes to your mind. Again, don't think about it, just let the first thing that comes to your mind make its way on paper. And again.

That's it. Do this once a week or once a month, whenever you feel like it. I do it once a month in my bed, with my eyes closed and with my mind-voice. I know you might think that I could've avoided this entire chapter altogether by just stating this in the beginning and being done with it without the incredible number of words, but that wouldn't do it justice. Gratitude isn't only 'write stuff down', it's actual acknowledgement of your life. It's different from listening and hearing, it is actual understanding how amazing your life is and how beautiful you can make it because you are healthy!

Now let's answer this chapter's exercises:

Why should I practice gratitude? If I manage to practice gratitude, what will that realisation produce? What are the virtues that I will gain from practicing gratitude? What is my mission?

I should practice gratitude in order to see the positives in my life. We are all susceptible to falling in the negative web that makes us focus on our immediate stress, when life is so beautiful. Not to sound nihilistic, but we are literally on a moving rock in an infinite space, gliding around a hot star from where we can't even see the stack of paper on our desk that requires attention. We only live once and we can always change our surrounding, be it the city for better opportunities, the country for cultural reasons, or the continent for other motives. If we made a habit of basking in sadness then we need to break it, and the way to do that is by being grateful. The way to do that is to acknowledge and appreciate what we have, to appreciate that life could be even worse without what we have, and ***to appreciate that it isn't and that we are actually alright and in a position to pursue greatness***.

If I manage to practice gratitude, that realisation will produce peace. It will produce the necessary tranquillity to realise that there is a place to return home to, that there is food to be consumed, that there is water (clean water) to be had, and that there is a bed to sleep in and recharge. It will produce the soothing feeling that today is not the end, and that you can push again!

The virtues that I will gain from practicing gratitude are prudence, fortitude, and temperance.

My mission is to count the things that truly matter to me, to remember to be grateful for them, and to think about the ugly life I would have without them. It is easy to think of how miserable life is, and how poor you are, and how you want something new, and interesting. Generally speaking, it is easy to blame life. What isn't easy is to pick yourself up, to let go of the bad behaviour you know you have to let go, to discover your life goal, to make a plan that leads to you activating in your domain in five years' time, and to get to it. It is so easy to forget that you are healthy, and to not take it for granted. Try today to let go of the use of your right hand, and try to do something for 24 hours with only your left hand. Stop taking for granted your health, stop focusing on your misery, dust yourself off and move forward!

What to take away: Being grateful is an amazing way to go about your day. You wake up, thank God for another day, appreciate your health, your bed, your food, your house, your job. Appreciate the privilege of being able to change your life, to research your passion, to develop yourself in order to work in the domain you wish for in three or five years. And then you plan. And every day you don't act on your plan you will be hit by guilt, because guilt stems from knowing deep enough that you could be better than the action that triggered the guilty feeling, and that action is ungratefulness (because if you were truly grateful, you'd work for yourself almost every day).

WHO DO YOU WANT TO BE?

FOREGONE

Chapter Φ

KNOW WHO YOU WANT TO BE

To find yourself, think for yourself.
— SOCRATES

WHO DO YOU WANT TO BE?

Life is such a wonderful gift, and we can make it even more wonderful by having the right guidance, be it early on or later down the journey. We have this amazing body that can sustain so much stress and damage, and recuperate afterwards miraculously.

We also have this amazing mind that has accomplished so many feats such as medicine, instant international communication, creating an enormous online library, and other vast accomplishments.

Last, but not least, we have the blessing to be born in this day and age. Would it be not a shame to let the passing of time and the dusk of age set upon us and instil regret? Regret of all the time we wasted, of the opportunities we missed, of the invitations we declined? It would, for if we look at the old masters of philosophy, of war, of art, of literature, all of them possess the same rough message: *the pain of discipline is but a grain compared to the pain of regret*. And thus we must turn to ourselves, the ones reading this book, the ones actively deciding to change our life for the better and to ask: shall we begin?

I must state that I don't like to assume but right now I will make an exception for you and assume the following: *you are a good person.* Your intentions stem from a good place, you have other people in mind, you like to help, and you are sometimes sad about the absent or decaying good in this world. If I've got at least two of them right then that's fine by me. You see, alike a pack of wolves, we are who we surround ourselves with, and thus you are a smoker if you surround yourself with smokers, and you are an athlete if you surround yourself with athletes. If you want to be sad then listen to sad people, and if you want to be happy then surround yourself with cheerful people. But know that that's not who you *truly* are, deep down.

Just because you mimic the behaviour of those around you doesn't mean that that's who you truly are. Who you are is something that only you alone can find, at home, in your own time and in your own head space. I allow myself again to assume and I say this: most people in their early 20's are generally similar, for they rarely know what they want and where they're headed. However, people past their mid-20's and in their 30's who read this book have either had (or will have) the knowing-and-forming-of-character-phase come in play, and that's because they have had the necessary experiences to form an idea of what they like and what they don't, and they have probably dealt with stress, loss, fury, anger, and other emotions that can easily lead to giving up on caring about others, and even about themselves.

But we must make sure to not fall in that pit, or to quickly get out before we get swallowed because life is really a juxtaposition of beauty and pain, and in the end it's up to us to make it work, and we have the means to do so! We have the power to try, to rearrange our thinking, our approach, our behaviour! I said before that I believe you to be a good person, and that is why I write this book: for you, for me, and for all the other good but depressed people out there who want to make a change, but either don't know where to start or they 'can't'. YES YOU CAN! This world is evil, and it will be your biggest enemy, it will beat you to the ground and it will keep you there if you let it. I had bouts of depression and months where the eyes were open but nobody was home, I had dark thoughts and basically the full package of depression, and yet I managed to turn it around eventually, and you can too!

By the time you're reading this book you probably have 50 or 40 more years to live, and in this time you *must* realise how much capacity to confront evil you have, and to realise the potential you have! You *must* think about what you truly want from life and also think about what around you isn't right and fix it! We are quick to judge ourselves as failures without ever really trying in the first place because we are prisoners to the *illusion of progress*.

How many times did you actually get up, made a list of the small addictions you have like watching too much tv, leaving the dishes for tomorrow, not making your bed, eating sweets every day, drinking sugary drinks, standing too much at your desk, not studying when you know you should, jumping over work for a night out with the gang, wasting time instead of working on your business or life goal, and actually worked on them?

How many times did you work on discovering what your true passion is, on what your true life ambition is, on trying new things in order to discover whether your soul actually likes that or not, whether baseball or basketball or drawing or cooking is your actual preferred way of using your time, and making it your life goal and maybe even your business?

How many times did you actually think about the true reason behind your motivation to act upon your true passion and realise that maybe the reason you quit is because that reason was not strong enough, or maybe you quit because you were doing the right thing, but for the wrong cause, or simply because motivation isn't everything, but discipline is?

How many times have you opened your calendar and made a schedule that prioritised your goals, declaring what's urgent and what can be left for the end of the day, as opposed to simply standing around choosing a colour to write the title and the date with for 15 minutes?

How many times did you actually give it a try for six months minimum with a full-on schedule, proper diet, rest, and goals before you gave up and called yourself a failure?

You *must* realise that you need to ask yourself questions, not demand answers of yourself. You have to treat yourself the way you'd want someone else to treat you, that is the secret. You have the lessons from your past, the actions of your present and the aiming of the future, and with some guidance you can realise your full potential. The problem appears when you think you are pursuing your potential by making unjust schedules for yourself, schedules where you work and study for 12 hours with minimum reward. That is a tried and tested recipe that'll make you want to stay as far away from your potential as possible! Nobody likes to be slaved, so why are you a slave to yourself? Why are you both your own bad employer and your own bad employee?

In demanding answers you can only think of the things you've done, and your logic is limited, but in asking questions you allow yourself to think outside the box, to hierarchically pursue a wave of thoughts that lead to implementation of a goal, and eventually to changing your perception and behaviour. Do we not get happy when we are motivated, and are we not motivated when we decide on a goal? Thus, the solution to a chaotic behaviour must come under the form of a question: if today I am just as sad as yesterday, what can I change so that tomorrow I'm happier?

You have the power inside of you, the conscience and the intuition to pursue greatness, to pull yourself up from the ground, to dust yourself off and to move forward. You have the power to get a job, save some money, and move out of town and out of the stress created by family, 'friends', or a bad neighbourhood if you really want to, whilst working on a side-business for yourself. You have to keep moving forward, and the steps below will assist you in doing just that. I believe in you, and I wish you good luck on the path!

What to take away: Knowing yourself is like drawing. Only by looking at last year's art do you realise the mistakes you've made and how far you've come!

Chapter 1
THE NERVOUS SYSTEM

Hope is evaluation of probability.
— ALEX IOVU

PURPOSE

The purpose of this chapter attempts to highlight the importance of having a well-rested nervous system, to present possible issues, and to explain the benefits of adopting a behaviour that benefits your nervous system.

INTROSPECTIVE

Remember the reason I gave in the *Introduction* chapter for writing this book? I said that I do not *have* a nervous system, *I am* a nervous system. This too is a double entendre, for although it might seem like a joke, I stand by it wholeheartedly.

Have you noticed how easy it is to pursue nobility and to keep on track with your plans, schedules, and goals when you're well rested? If yes, have you ever questioned yourself about the reason behind that? No worries if you didn't, because that's exactly what we'll discuss about in this chapter.

DEFINE

What is *the nervous system? The nervous system* is the complex system that coordinates actions and information by sending and receiving signals to and from different parts of the body. The nervous system maintains homeostasis.

Homeostasis is the ability of a living organism to adjust its internal environment in order to maintain dynamic constancy. The word is derived from the ancient Greek words 'homoios' (same), and 'stasis' (steady). Although it means steady and same, it doesn't mean it's static, but that it's moving in-between values.

You see, nothing in life stays the same, and that applies outside of philosophy too. Our body works in-between defined parameters that have a margin allowance. Although our temperature is supposed to be 37C, we can go one degree higher or lower.

On top of that, homeostasis is brought back to 'normal' values by negative-feedback-mechanisms (NFM), or positive-feedback-mechanisms (PFM). So if you get too cold, the body starts shivering in order to warm itself up (NFM). If you cut yourself, the body starts making blood platelets in order to patch the cut (PFM). Everything has parameters, and when the system is disturbed, it works to bring everything back to 'normal', and that is taxing on the system, as you can't make a fire without wood.

In case you think you know this, or question the point of it, are you aware that you do not apply in your day-to-day life all that you know to be beneficial to you, especially these 'general known facts'? And even if you do, are you sure your behaviour is positively impacting your nervous system?

The reason I ask this is because hearing and understanding are not one and the same. Remember that we sometimes listen to answer, instead of listening to understand. Just because you know something to be beneficial, that doesn't mean you'll also implement it into your active behaviour.

The easiest way to verify if a general known fact you know is active knowledge is by looking at your actions: when you truly know something, you make your world revolve around that which you know. So if you know that the pan is hot, then you make sure to never touch it without a glove, or at all. Based on this, just because you know that it is recommended to have a well-rested nervous system, that doesn't mean that you will make the necessary adjustments to your behaviour to achieve that.

Why? Probably because you don't see the benefits of it (first stage of competence), or because nobody talked to you about it, or because you prefer instant gratification as opposed to delayed gratification. As a former biology and chemistry student (although I studied these sciences only in the first two years of university), it would be my pleasure to open your eyes to the benefits of a well-rested nervous system.

You see, your *philosophy of life* consists of everything you believe and know to be true and helpful to your daily life. Your philosophy is the sum of your actions, be it the fruits you choose to eat based on what you read, the oil you choose to use based on your research, the position you have at your desk, etc. Your philosophy will show whether this information about the nervous system you 'know' is general knowledge, or whether you actually understand it: if you have dark circles around your eyes, get mad easily, feel depressed and without energy, lost and without motivation to search, and instead of addressing it you dive into distractions to hide your suffering in the same way a child hides dirt under the rug in order to avoid responsibility, then let me tell you, you do not understand it. You only know it. Let's begin understanding it.

ILLUSTRATE

Since getting mad, assuming, being aggressive/passive are easier to occur when we are tired, and we know them to be bad, then the opposite of all that is when we are rested and we are good, peaceful, and happy. We've already discussed peace in the previous section, and now we will address happiness. Happiness and good mood is given by a number of factors, such as endorphins, dopamine, and serotonin. All are substances *produced and released **by our body*** (emphasis on *released*).

On one hand, endorphins are chemicals that reduce pain and relieve stress. Although these are known to usually release when doing exercise, that is not the only case. We also release endorphins when we listen to music, when we create art, when we laugh, when we dance, basically whenever we engage our artistic side, but not only.

On the other hand, dopamine and serotonin are the chemicals that trigger excitement, good mood, and happiness itself:

- Dopamine is the hormone of good-mood, generally speaking. Not necessarily happiness, but good-mood overall. It is triggered by the same activities that trigger endorphins.
- Serotonin is the hormone of happiness. The next chapter is entirely dedicated to happiness, so I'll save the surprise.

So if these are our chemicals, then based on the fact that we have control over our mind, and therefore our choices, we can engage in behaviour that releases them, like training, eating better, sleeping well, etc. Based on this, take a second to ask yourself: 'what is there to gain from not releasing these chemicals?'. Answer truthfully before jumping to the next section.

REWARD

Stress. That is the reward. Actual, constant stress.

We might not even have any problems in our lives, and be bugged by this constant feeling of our head exploding, our focus not sharp, angry for no reason, depressed, and moody. Like darkness is the absence of light, so too is stress the absence of happiness.

Just like maintaining a clean house is easier than doing a general clean-up every Sunday, so too is the body's ability to maintain stability easier than to rock back and front in-between extremities. So how can you hope to maintain homeostasis and to release your endorphins, dopamine, and serotonin if you don't ever clean your house? If you do not exercise, if you have poor sleep, poor diet, smoke, and unhinge your jaw like a snake to consume alcohol? (Note that these are not the only thing required for happiness, so good job if you sleep well, eat well, train well!)

That is why I said that the emphasis is on the word *released,* for we have what is required to be in a good mood, and the power to choose to engage in activities that release those chemicals. It's like the fire and the wood I mentioned. Since the wood (actions) doesn't get itself, it's time to cut some trees (make some choices).

ANALYSE

On top of that, everything in life has tension, and reacts to the tensile strength (the maximum load that can be supported without fracture). If we imagine our nervous system to be a balloon,, then in our case the tension is measured by how well-rested the nervous system is.

The nervous system can be negatively-stressed (and its tensile strength exceeded) by a number of factors:

- Lack of sleep. The nervous system gets tense and flexes when you lack sleep. The more flexed it is, the easier it is for us to lose patience, temperance, composure. Remember how you grind your teeth and snap at everything when you're super tired. Lack of sleep inflates the balloon.
- Lack of proper diet. Everything in life is chemistry that studies biology with the help of mathematics. That's it. How do you expect to feel good if feeling good is brought on by homeostasis, and you don't touch the parameters defined by homeostasis with your diet? You think those vitamins and minerals are a joke? Lack of diet inflates the balloon.
- Lack of hydration. We are 70% water, give or take. Water is the base substance for all of our chemical actions, reactions, and exchanges. How can we function properly without proper hydration? Lack of hydration inflates the balloon.
- Lack of temperance. Fast-food, alcohol, processed snacks, and sweets in moderation (one item, finger-size quantity, once per week) will never kill you (I hope not), but excess abuse of the liver, the pancreas, and the adrenal glands will. Our body is a muscle, and just like we get tired mentally after long hours at the computer, and physically after a workout, so too do our organs tire. If you can't carry a heavy weight for a long time without putting it down, how can your body carry all that lack of temperance, and more importantly, for how long before it puts it down? Before it puts you down? Lack of temperance inflates the balloon.
- Combine this every day, and see how pop-goes-the-balloon. To do anything you must have energy, and if you lack energy because you don't drink water, eat coma-inducing-food (postprandial somnolence), are tired and snappy as a result of your lack of sleep,

then how do you expect to change your life? You don't *have* a nervous system, you *are* a nervous system.

UNDERSTAND

The nervous system is, among many things, a system that innervates muscles. The signal from your brain travels all the way to the muscles and instructs them to contract. Now the nervous system, like everything else, has a limit that is measured with a threshold. This threshold's intensity is reflected by your actions, and depending on the abuse you inflicted on it (by sleeping five hours a night, by having a bad diet, by drinking too much, by smoking, by being mad all the time, etc) or not, it will either be high, or low.

That is why you're snappier on days where you didn't sleep, didn't eat, and didn't hydrate well. On a bad day you can't even perform your best because you're nervous system isn't recharged properly, and it can't get rejuvenated without the active choice to change your chaotic lifestyle, to choose to have a behaviour that relaxes the nervous system so that tomorrow you can push with more strength. Thus, I have an exercise for you:

As mentioned in the first paragraph, one way of verifying the strength of your nervous system is through muscle contraction. You don't necessarily need to check *the absolute most exerted force you can exert (like a deadlift)*, but you need to check that *the force you exert every day is the same*. I want you to buy a notebook and an older weight scale model that has a tongue (NOT MADE OF GLASS or anything that can harm you).

Every morning when you wake up, I want you to 'check your weight', but instead of getting with your feet on it, I want you to grab the scale with both hands and lift it in front of you (like holding your hands on a driving wheel). Then, I want you to squeeze as hard as you can for four-to-five seconds. You can use the counter-force of your eight long fingers and press on it with your thumbs, that's how I do it.

Pay attention to the amount of force you exert on the scale (the amount of weight displayed by the tongue) in these four-to-five seconds. Do this every morning for a week, and write down in your notebook the amount of force showed every day (the weight displayed by the tongue). The reason for doing this is for you to check how well rested you are, and to make the necessary adjustments to get back on track if you aren't performing your best. Do this whenever you feel bad, and I mean really bad, like four-hours-of-sleep-triple-shot-espresso-bad.

OVERCOME

I don't think this needs to be dragged on much more, since most of the things but one are easy to explain: make sure to drink 2L of water every day, get *quality* sleep (an undisturbed 7-9 hour rest which, depending on each person, will be told by trial & error), make sure to do at least 30 minutes of fast walking every day, quit smoking or cut back, and moderate your alcohol intake to one 125ml glass of red wine per day, maybe one glass every two days actually.

The elephant in the room is, of course, your diet. I cannot help you there, but I can guide you towards Google which, after searching for 'nutritionist course', will come up with plenty of opportunities, offers, and prices. Studying nutrition was one of the best choices of my life. Trust me, the best investment is the one you do for your health. Also, although I do not believe it, let's assume that this chapter managed to open your eyes to the benefits of a nervous system (the first stage of competence). You still have three steps to take, so start researching!

What to take away: The nervous system is the system that measures your performance. If today you are snappy and unfocused, you might want to start addressing that by resting better, eating better, reading or learning something, going for a walk, and relaxing with a movie or a game at the end of the day.

FOREGONE

Chapter 2

HAPPINESS IS THE JOURNEY, NOT THE DESTINATION

The meaning of life is to give life meaning.
— VIKTOR FRANKL

PURPOSE

The purpose of this chapter attempts to teach us how to be happy. Believe it or not, we can actually trigger happiness on command, chemically speaking!

INTROSPECTIVE

Marcus Aurelius says that we should take a good look at wise people's ruling principle. Just like a junior chef 'steals' knowledge by observing his senior and implementing his tips & tricks, so too should we improve ourselves by the work of others. If you want to discuss with the greatest minds of the previous centuries, then go to a library and pick up their writings.

Even if you have modern-day problems, most of them can be solved by looking at our judgement and adjusting our vices, and all the steps to changing one's behaviour can be found in the works of our predecessors, hence the first two sections of this book. And if your problem is a specific, modern-day problem? Then you look at the writings of the modern day specialists, or contact them. If we do not know history then we are doomed to repeat it, thus wisdom is power!

DEFINE

What is *happiness*? *Happiness* is that state of smiling until your cheeks hurt, that state of feeling like you're slightly lifting off the ground, that state of thinking you're incredible and can overcome anything. *Happiness* is a chemical inside us that we can learn to activate!

We have a saying in my country: 'God gives you, but he doesn't bag it for you'. Hopefully this sends the message that you have everything that you need within you to succeed, but that you need to get up and get started. You need to understand that nothing is given for free, and that the world owes you nothing. You have to get up and work for it, and the way to do that is by understanding more about yourself with the help of neuropsychology and chemistry.

First of all, neuropsychology is the branch of psychology that studies the nervous system. Since the central nervous system is composed of the brain and the spine, neuropsychology studies the relationship between the brain and its behaviour. We will only focus on one area, and that is the brain's frontal lobe. This area deals with executive functions such as planning, organising, and initiating, among other, and it is activated by your choice to plan, organise, or initiate something. Shocker!

Second of all, although produced in the brain, when looking closer at our gastrointestinal tract we can see a little neurotransmitter called serotonin. This neurotransmitter is known for its ability to make us happy, more dominant, and less aggressive. This hormone is (also) triggered by the activation of the frontal lobe, i.e. you planning to start studying *regularly,* or to *regularly* do physical exercises, or any other *daily scheduled activity* that will better your overall existence.

Based on this, we can note that serotonin will not activate if you do not have a goal, and since serotonin is literally the *happiness* chemical, that you will be miserable as a result, correct?

ILLUSTRATE

Humans are driven by challenges and actions. We are not made to Netflix & chill, but instead we are made to be active. We are predators, and that can be seen by looking at the position of our eyes, which isn't on the side like prey who needs to see the surrounding danger, but forward. The true spark of life is found in challenges, and not in distractions such as:

- Playing games for 12 hours a day just so you can avoid the harsh reality that your life is, which is that you're purposeless and depressed. So much easier to forget that and dive into distractions, right? Remember that distractions are not happiness, they are just that. Distractions. (me)
- Listening to your friends tell you how 'you're perfect the way you are', which is an absolute lie. You're not perfect, you're miserable! You don't want to hear that toxic positivity, you want change! (me)
- Being ungrateful and sitting in bed, crying because of how bad your 'circumstances' are, and how life is unfair and got you in this loop. No! You got yourself in, and you can get yourself out! (me)

'Alright that's great, but what does predator, gratitude, and happiness have in common?', you ask. At surface level it might seem like nothing, so keep on reading and you will understand how being grateful is for the predator what fuel is for the engine.

We all know how we feel when we finish a task, right? Relaxed, relieved, but nevertheless empty because we now have to search for something else to do. I myself, maybe because of ADHD too, must always be on the move. Must always learn something. I feel... I'm purposelessly floating through existence when I'm not doing anything.

Based on this, take a second to ask yourself: 'what is there to gain from not pursuing anything in life?'. Answer truthfully before jumping to the next section.

REWARD

Torment. That is the reward.

As mentioned in the previous chapter, we need to prove ourselves. Maybe because we are animals, and as part of a society we tend to show our dominant skills in order to not be challenged, and to assert dominance. Maybe because we genetically understand that, as animals, we need a good partner to reproduce with, and if we want the best partner then we need to be the best partner. Whatever the reason may be, we always have the need to do something, and 9 out of 10 times (especially when doing it for ourselves), we have the need to do it perfect.

So how can we be better at *doing nothing?* How can we show our skills when we *do nothing?* I'm not talking about things like meditation, don't get cheeky, I'm specifically talking about not pursuing a goal. We can't. Don't believe me? Go do a five day movie marathon. No, scratch that, do a three day movie marathon. You'd start happy and get bored mid-way. I have many examples, but they all end the same. You'd get bored of everything you'd do that doesn't lead to productivity. To challenges. To that spark of 'what now? This is interesting, I don't know how to do this, so let's find out!'.

ANALYSE

The reason I say this is because happiness is the chemical *serotonin*, and that activates when you have a goal and pursue it. So even if you win the lottery and go on a maniacal shopping spree of house, car, and things you buy that you don't need, you won't be happy a month after because you're stuck doing nothing, you're pathless, purposeless.

All generations that have had the following experience went through the feeling of not being as happy as they were previously after some time elapsed since the purchase: remember how we placed our new phone down gently for the first month, and then just randomly threw it on our bed a month after? That feeling you have when you sit on your couch, your chair, or your bed will be the same feeling you will have a month after sitting on a better version of furniture. When you sit down in front of your new expensive television, on your hand-made-custom-tailored-Egyptian-cotton bed, and when you'll think about what you want to do with your life will be the moment when you will realise and truly understand what misery is. What being a predator without any prey is. You'll understand that for all the things you possess, you have nothing. You can turn your expensive state-of-the-art television on and off, you can play a videogame, you can go to the market to buy stuff, but in the end you are just floating through existence. Purposeless. You're nothing more than a robot that does the minimum requirements to *exist*, but do you **live**?

FOREGONE

UNDERSTAND

Viktor Frankl says that 'when a person can't find a deep sense of meaning they distract themselves with pleasure', and that is another universal truth. Ask yourself about your purpose: 'what is my purpose? What is my point in life?'.

No matter how much money you spend, ***you can't be happy and feel pointless at the same time!*** When you distract yourself you're not actually happy, you're just occupied, and the sooner you understand this the faster you'll get to changing your life. Happiness is not found in things, only comfort. Happiness is found within yourself. Alike a wolf, happiness is found in the idea of hunting, killing, eating. Happiness is found in the ability to achieve. Happiness is found in the journey, not in the moment you get home after the journey ended and the time is past. You're not happy then, you're satisfied. Happiness is something different!

The wolf doesn't care if it eats its trophy on snow or on a hand-made-custom-tailored-Egyptian-cotton bed, it just is happy for the thrill of the hunt. That is why it is important to have a goal, a challenge, something to look forward to, as opposed to playing games all day, or just crying over things you can't control. Happiness is when we're hungry and we put distractions aside, such as the phone ringing, and we start preparing our food. Happiness is when we take that first bite and that last bite. Immediately after, the thrill of the hunt is over. After we eat we aren't happy, we're satisfied.

OVERCOME

'Great, so how do I become happy?', you ask.

You focus on these three chapters:

- Current one: you understand *the frontal lobe* and *serotonin*. You understand the importance of a plan, and that without making a plan that will manifest your dream into reality you can't be *truly* happy.
- The next one: you use *the creative process*. You must have a purpose, something to guide you, otherwise you'll have many moments of doubt, anxiety, and existential crises. Where are you headed?

- The one after the next one: you find an answer to the question *'why?'*. Avoiding a task in favour of comfort is no news to us, we've all done it. That is why it is important to have a reason to not give up on pursuing your purpose. To have a reason that is so strong, no amount of comfort can tempt you!

Also keep in mind that, like a videogame, the end is eclipsed by the journey, and that's because the end is only a conclusion of everything that has been done. There is nothing to achieve there. The game just ends. Nobody starts a game thinking 'boy I can't wait to finish this game and be done with it'.

Thus, the journey is the most important, and I can prove this easily by reminding you about how good you felt when you were in the middle of pursuing a task, and how that sense of victory that came with the completion of the task also came with a sense of wondering, a sense of *'now what?'*.

Pursuing the end would be counterproductive because there's nothing there. The game closes when the end is reached, and that's the counterproductive part, the *'now what?'* part. That is why it is a general known truth that the most important part of the life is the journey itself, and the joy brought by learning the skills, by overcoming the challenges, and by being better every day!

What to take away: After using *the creative process (next chapter)* and finding that one thing that you can't wait to get back to, it's time to make a plan! It's time to organise your schedule and include at least one or two hours for the activity that you discovered talks to your soul, and to do it every day! The reason for that is because your brain's frontal lobe, after being activated by you making a plan, triggers serotonin, and serotonin is happiness!

Chapter 3
THE CREATIVE PROCESS

Though no one can go back and make a brand new start, anyone can start from now and make a brand new ending.
— CARL BARD

PURPOSE

The purpose of this chapter is to bring to attention that we have the necessary tools to be happy and purposeful, and yet we always look outside for help.

INTROSPECTIVE

Alright, I confess, I have been cheeky on that one. Of course we look outside for help, I wouldn't know anything if I didn't read others' books. But that's not what I meant. No, what I meant is that we never look at our inner selves for help. We ask others to give us purpose, to give us comfort, to give us value. It's time for that to change!

Before we dive in this chapter I'd like to ask you to note that *life is meant to be lived however we wish (as long as we morally respect others' boundaries)*, so if you're fine with your 9-to-5 job, then that's great! Some people never question their purpose, they just work their job and have fun. That's enough for them, and to their standards that is perfect!

We all are different, and we all have different standards as a result. We shouldn't belittle others for not wanting to search for purpose, for knowledge, or anything else that *we think* is necessary for true happiness. Some people believe that you should be on an OMAD Keto diet and to have 5 PhD's, and that if you don't then you're not truly happy. That's not true, is it?

You're happy when you do what you like and want to do, not when you do what someone else's definition of happy is, and that is what this chapter's focus is about: finding that which makes *you* happy! There is no book left by God Himself that says that your purpose should be this, or that, or anything at all! You can be an artist, a scientist, a constructor, whatever you wish, and for those of us that have questions, for those of us that are not alright with wasting time, with wasting potential, with wasting the knowledge of our predecessors, and ultimately with wasting life itself: I get you, and I got you! I will do my best to share with you the steps that I use right now to pursue every day with maximum effort.

DEFINE

What is *the creative process*? *The creative process* is the process we use to discover our passion. It is the simple process of experimenting with an art or science subject for at least a week, on my recommendation, in order to discover a potential hidden passion. I recommend trying something new for at least a week because excitement usually wears out in four to seven days.

We all know what excitement feels like, we've all gotten a new phone, a new television, or something we wanted, used it for a week, and then went back to our regular mood. In order to avoid that and to check truthfully the validity of our feelings, more than a week is recommended when trying out something new.

I have searched for purpose my entire life. I tried to be an athlete, to play basketball, to do photorealistic art, anime art, 3D art, to study chemistry, biology, nutrition, and so on and so forth. The list is endless. I even reached points where I thought I finally got it, only to realise that I was wrong, to discard it, and to go back to searching. As bad as it sounds, know that I never lost hope, and I was rewarded for that because not all was in vain eventually. It all helped finetune the searching process, and finally led to discovering my one true passion.

FOREGONE

ILLUSTRATE

Since Corona virus pandemic started to make its presence known in Europe, early March 2020, I decided to leave Great Britain and to move to Greece. Here I had my father, here there were little-to-no-virus-cases, here I had peace and time to think, away from the big and loud city that London is. Here is where I began my real life.

The shops in Greece usually close in-between 14:00 to 16:30, as people like to rest. My father had some time to kill and asked me if I want to go for ice-cream. As we were sitting and talking, he brought up the subject of purpose. He asked me about my life purpose, about what I see myself doing. I said that I have always engaged in some sort of exercise, be it either gym, calisthenics, running, and that I wanted to activate in that domain.

He nodded and asked me 'and if that doesn't work?'. I said that it's no problem, because I have my nutrition expertise, and that I can always make money with nutrition. He asked me again: 'and if that doesn't work?'. I said that it's also no problem, because I can work in a gym since I also have personal trainer expertise. He asked me again: 'and if that doesn't work?'. I said that it's fine, since I have some money saved with which I can open up a swim-shorts company, we live at the beach after all. He asked me again: 'and if that doesn't work?'. I said that I can always find a job here at the local businesses.

Based on this, take a second to ask yourself: 'what is there to gain from not questioning what I'm truly interested in?'. Answer truthfully before jumping to the next section.

REWARD

Existential crisis. This is the reward.

Before torment comes the existential crisis. That feeling of the world being big, and we being small. The world being full, and us being empty. It's that feeling that there are so many things to do, and yet none for us.

An existential crisis can happen at any time, and with different intensities. It usually occurs as we advance in age and we notice the people around us working on something, be it a personal project or at a big company. We start asking questions about our future, about where we are heading, about who we want to be, and other philosophical questions.

The thing that triggers it is at first, in my opinion, the need to participate or to belong. It's the need to not be left behind, to move with the world. Even if that is or it isn't the case, the second (or first) thing that triggers it is doubt. 'Are we really that weak to not find our purpose? Are we really that stupid that we have no talent? Are we really not good at anything?'. Whatever the reason behind this occurrence, there is a solution. Keep reading.

ANALYSE

This conversation occurred again and again over a period of two months. It was actually a little bit stressing to always answer the same question with the same answer. I felt like something was amiss, but I also knew my father asks a lot of questions, so I paid no mind. I just figured he was so busy with clients, documents and what else that he just forgot we talked about this. But at a certain point all this questioning started to get to me and to open my mind to things I didn't think about before, such as:

- Why is he fixated on this subject? Is he trying to tell me something?
- Now that he mentions it, I have so many plans, but why?
- Do I really want to rely on them, or are they some sort of a fail-safe plans?
- Do my fail-safe plans actually have meaning to me?
- How strong do I feel about them?
- Do I see myself doing any of them forever if my main one doesn't work?
- Which even is my main one, and which is a fail-safe?
- Which one do I feel like doing for the rest of my life?

I started to '*clean my room*', to make order in my thoughts, to ask myself about my desires. What do I desire? What is my future goal? Why do I have so many fail-safe plans? Am I really so afraid to truly pursue something that I need to have a fail-safe plan? Am I really so undisciplined that I can't make up my mind, that I can't make a routine?

If I had all the money and time in the world, what would I see myself doing for the rest of my life?

UNDERSTAND

The subject of purpose popped up again at our following conversation. I told him that I want to activate in the fitness industry, as I always did, to put to work my nutrition studies and my personal training studies, and to make a life for myself. I want to be a good influence and to help people find themselves, just like I was helped by people like Mike Thurston, Christian Poulos, Ryan Serhant, Ian Somerhalder, Jordan B. Peterson, etc.

When he asked me 'and if that doesn't work?', I told him that it will work, and that it cannot *not work*. He asked me why I say that, and I replied that I can't allow myself to think that it won't work. I can't allow myself to have a plan B because that means that I do not believe in my plan strong enough, and if I don't believe in it, I won't put my full effort into it. I told him that it will work, and I believe in myself. We never spoke about this subject again.

It is to my understanding that he noticed me struggling, and acted accordingly. He asked me questions and pushed until I started to actively think about them on my own. Remember that we shouldn't demand answers from ourselves, but we should ask questions. Questioning commences the mind's creative mode.

Thus began again *the creative process,* the final one I believe. I sat down and I thought about my future:

- I thought about the destination I'm heading towards: fitness.
- I thought about the specific branch I want to take: bodybuilding.
- I thought about the answer to the question why: feel well mentally.
- I thought about the goal: passive incomes & Dubai every winter.
- I thought about the fail-safe plans: I stopped lying to myself.

- I thought about a new behaviour: dropped most time-wasting addictions.

In three words: *questioning and planning*. This was the key to success, and in the following two chapters we will see why!

OVERCOME

'Alright, so I use *this creative process*, the process where I start exploring a subject for more than a week. What then?', you ask. It's simple. You get started on something, you listen to your soul, and you search deep for that 'I can't wait to do this again' feeling. It's as simple as that.

First of all, *you look at yourself and you ask yourself: 'what do I find myself mostly attracted to?'*. Think broadly, you'll zoom in later. A tip that might work for you is to try and recall the things you do when you're bored, for that is usually when your passion secretly comes out. Are you attracted to art, or to science? Do you find yourself drawing random things when you're bored, or do you go listen to youtubers talk about molecules, blackholes and what else? Think about which of the two you're more attracted to, art or science, and answer truthfully.

Second of all, *after declaring your preferred domain, take a pen and paper and write down five things you want to try from that respective domain*. Say, for example, if you're more into art, you could try following Gordon Ramsay on YouTube, look at some of his recipe video guides, buy the ingredients, and start cooking one meal a day! Or maybe open up a cartoon or tv show you grew up with, and try to draw the main character!

Third of all, *experiment for at least a week with something, and then move on if no feelings occur!* So you liked cooking, but it isn't your gig, and after a week you're kind of tired. No problem, get a pen and paper, open up your pc, look at some cartoons or movies you love, pause them, and try to draw that exact scene. Or take baseball lessons, or go to the stadium and find a gymnast coach. Whatever you decided on doing, do it for at least a week. See if your soul responds to it.

MEMENTO MORI

"You could leave life right now. Let that determine what you do and say and think."
- Marcus Aurelius

Lastly, as a Stoicism student, I would like to bring to attention the quote *Memento Mori* (Latin for 'remember you are mortal'). Look at the previous image (feel free to use it for personal use). The first column represents the average life-span of a person, which is 80 years old. Each horizontal box is a week. Since there are 52 weeks in a year, there are 52 boxes. Although this might seem nihilistic, it isn't. It's the opposite. If nihilistic people have no responsibility since they believe that life has no meaning, we Stoicism students have responsibility since we know that life has meaning, and the meaning is *to pursue virtue and wisdom,* as our Stoic forefathers put it.

Assuming life goes well, you and I have the same amount of time on this planet, give or take. Therefore we can agree that at the end of a month we can have 31 excuses, or 31 achievements, correct? We can agree that at the end of a year we have about 40 missed one-and-a-half-weeks-creative-process-experiments, or 40 things we have tried, correct? The time will still pass, regardless if you found your purpose or gave up.

Time waits for no one, and the more you wait, the harder it gets. Socrates says that 'It is a shame for a man to grow old without seeing the beauty and strength of which his body is capable.'

You only live once, so what better things do you have to do than to try and be the best at that which you excel at? Do you have anything better to do? Do you really? What do you have to do? You can't change the past since it's gone, and you can't change the future since it didn't happen yet, and that's where the secret lies! You have control over your future and can influence it by focusing on the current moment! Remember that the person you are today is the person you've formed yourself over the past 5 years. One day at a time, so go out there and push forward! I believe in you!

What to take away: The only way to get out if you're stuck is to start moving. You can't work with nothing, but you can work with something, so pick a side, be it either art or science, choose a branch, and start experimenting!

Chapter 4
THE PRINCIPLE OF THE QUESTION 'WHY?'

By failing to prepare you are preparing to fail.
— BENJAMIN FRANKLIN

PURPOSE

The subject of this chapter pertains to your purpose, and it attempts to make you realise that you must question yourself about the reason you chose to pursue your goal, and about the strength of your answer. Is it a good answer? Are you motivated enough by it? Is it the one, true answer? Did you search within enough?

INTROSPECTIVE

It is very important to have a powerful reason behind everything you do, not only behind the answer to the previous chapter. As you will learn in the next chapters, a plan and a schedule are very important for your life. Your frontal lobe has the executive function of planning, scheduling, and organizing, and you trigger serotonin when you plan and schedule something.

Serotonin is the chemical of happiness. That is why happiness is the path, not a place you're going to reach one day: because you can't have serotonin in your system without having a plan, or in layman's terms, because you can't be happy without a destination. Neuropsychologically speaking.

Based on this we can conclude that we first need to find out what we want to do with our life by using *the creative process*, and like a weapon we hone, fortify our life goal with a powerful reason that keeps us on track.

'But why do we need to have a powerful reason behind what we do?', you ask. Because of these two letters: IQ. *Intelligence Quotient* is how we measure a person's reasoning ability. A higher IQ doesn't signify that a person will be great, it just represents the potential of a person's capability to be great. At the end of the day we are still humans, and we can still be victims to distractions, addictions, laziness, and other time-consuming behaviour, regardless if our IQ has two digits or three.

Simply put, we need to have a reason for our purpose because we all have a limit to how much reasoning we can output, and also because we need to know and to be reminded from time to time of why we do what we do. Just because you found out what you're good at doesn't mean you'll get up and do it. How many times did you skip work to pursue other activities? How many times did you order food instead of cooking? How many times did you watch television instead of studying? Get it?

That is why we must have a reason behind what we do. We need to be reminded that we have an aim, that there is a reward, and that we can either have excuses or progress, but not both.

DEFINE

What is *the principle of the question 'why?'*? The principle of *the question 'why?'* is the motivation that stands behind our actions. It is the reason that makes us get up from our bed and cook, clean, wash, work, train, etc. It is the scale that balances *the energy we use to complete an action*, and *the reward we receive upon completion.*

What is *willpower?* When looking at this word it would be better to separate it in two to reach a deeper understanding:

- *Will* is the wish to act upon the world, be it either to wish to open our eyes, or to wish to run for president. It is our desire. Our covet.
- *Power* is the tool we use to measure the intensity of the *will*. So we might have the *will* to quit smoking, but the *power* to do so is so low

that we give in to our need to buy a pack of cigarettes. This is why it is important to have a well-rested nervous system.

'Why is it important to have an answer to the question 'why?'?', you ask. Let me explain with a small example about a gym friend who today of all days is feeling a little off in the confidence department. Our friend is doubting his abilities, and asks: 'why should I continue to go to the gym? There are thousands of others who are better looking than me! I'll never make a dent in the industry! I quit!'.

That right there is an example of losing focus on the answer to the question 'why?', if he even had one to begin with. The individual weighted the amount of confidence possessed in that particular moment against the possibility of being amongst the greatest, and got instantly humbled and crushed under the weight of it. That is why we use short-term, medium-term, and long-term goals when approaching a task (more in the chapter *The illusion of progress*). You look at each stair individually, not at the staircase itself. You watch the step in front of you, you don't focus on the top of the mountain, otherwise you slip because you aren't paying attention to your steps.

ILLUSTRATE

This book is like a baby to me. It is my legacy, it is who I am. It is my naked soul. It is egoless (I hope). I think I would lose it if were to lose it. You can always write again, but the time you spent finetuning and whittling away every sentence into industrial-standards-quality? Sheesh. It's like never saving in Photoshop and losing five days of work from a power outage.

So what pushes me to write this book? What is my answer to the question 'why?'?. When I ask myself 'why do I want to write a book?', I answer that I write because I want to help others who, unlike me, haven't stumbled yet upon these lessons. I have always considered myself a self-sacrificing-Samaritan-martyr who cares only about the ones around me, and I prove this to myself day after day.

I never thought about writing a book, and yet when I think about all the good I can do by sharing some lessons that helped pull me back from the edge, my soul smiles and I get to work.

Based on this, take a second to ask yourself: 'what is there to gain from not questioning the reasons behind whatever I plan on doing?'. Answer truthfully before jumping to the next section.

REWARD

Amotivation. Worst case scenario, even avolition. That low willpower, that dragging of feet, that procrastination, that avoidance of responsibility. That is the reward.

It's the lying-in-bed-with-your-eyes-half-open sensation, looking at the ceiling and asking yourself what's the point of getting up. That's why it is said that *if your dream doesn't scare you it isn't for you.* Because when you don't have a strong answer to the question 'why am I doing this?', not only do you have low willpower, but you also have a lack of fear of consequences. A lack of fear to miss even one day, a lack of fear to not be better than you were yesterday. You can waste weeks or months, and that time isn't coming back, and even worse, that time could've been used to get you closer to where you want to be.

That is why it's important to have a good answer to the question 'why?'. Because where you are right now isn't good, and nobody likes to be there, but in order to not suffer anymore one day, you have to motivate yourself by thinking of that magnificent day that will come, and to push towards it!

ANALYSE

There is something so nice in being kind, in seeing someone smile and be relieved of their hardship because you helped. In doing the right thing and giving it your best for the benefit of others, without any need and expectation of reward.

Based on that statement we can interpret that 'helping others' is what drives me. Thus, if I were to have chosen a lesser answer to the question 'why?', I probably wouldn't have pulled through and delivered the book. Why is that? Because I simply have no passion for writing itself.

FOREGONE

I'm not trying to find something to say because I like to write, but because I have something to say I write.

UNDERSTAND

There is an equation that I think we are all aware of subconsciously when it comes to understanding purpose and reasoning.

The first half of the equation is that everything we do must be validated/approved by our willpower, and willpower is like a muscle: it gets tired after using it. *Bad choices such as late-night sleep, poor diet, stress, alcohol, smoking, and other negative-nervous-system-stressing-behaviours lead to a decrease in willpower,* which consequently leads to losing focus of the things that matter. Losing focus on the answer to the question 'why?' can lead to minor mistakes that, if accumulated over time, can lead to complacency, excess comfort relaxation, and other unruliness.

The second half of the equation says that behind everything we do in life there must be a reason (assuming that our willpower is in good shape). The quality of the reason impacts the quality of the outcome. Thus, if the reason we come up with is mediocre, then we shall give up pursuing our ambition, whilst if it is average then we might give it a chance and give up halfway through the journey. Please note that you could have the best reason in the world and still fail to do something. There are things for which we are not meant, such as I am not meant for mathematics and, although I understand it, I would never pursue it. That is why I stress the importance of *the creative process.*

OVERCOME

Let's do a recap:

- We're all good at something. There is something for everyone out there, and the way to discover it is by using *the creative process.* The process requires you to choose between art and science, and to write down five activities from that domain (be it art, sculpture, cooking, photography, and video editing, or studying chemistry, biology, physics, physiology, or philosophy). After that, you must pick something and start doing it for more than a week, one hour a day. Study chemistry, make plasteline sculptures, read philosophy, etc.

- Once you discover that which you think is your purpose, you must make sure to search for an answer to the following question: 'but why do I want to do it?'. This answer helps in the days when you will be tested, and you will be tested by the four stages of competence. This answer's function is to stabilize you when you tremble on the path. When you want to give in to wasting another day, another week, another month.

'Alright great, so how do I find my answer to the question 'why?'? How do I get to pass the first stage of competence?', you ask.

First of all, *we start by defining what a purpose is*. A purpose is a being's reason to exist. Everything in life has a purpose. As a tree has the purpose to grow and to make fruit, so too does everything else in life serves a purpose. As conscient beings, we should be searching for our purpose, our 'why?', and *that is because we can have the best boat in the world, but waste it by not having a destination*. Because we have *the privilege* to engage in behaviour that is not available to other beings, because we have *the privilege* to experience sensations that other beings don't experience, because we have *the privilege to have the privilege of conscience*. And if you don't find your purpose, you'll wake up one day and have an existential crisis, and the further advanced you are in age, the bigger the impact of the crisis will be.

Second of all, *we look at what a purpose does to us, and we define its benefits*. A purpose drives us, a purpose gives us meaning. A purpose is something we use when we are lost. Alike a map, we pull up our purpose and we regain direction. Alike a mother's embrace, we become invulnerable when everything around us crumbles. We gain focus, and we move forward.

Lastly, *you need to understand where and how to find it, and that is deep within you*. As much as I'd like to give you the steps, there are no steps. But do not be afraid, for although you seem to be on your own, you are not alone! I will help you by telling you what worked for me, and what I went through to discover my answer to the question 'why?', and that is *questioning*!

Questioning initiates the mind's creative behaviour, and it allows us to experiment with answers. Answers that can either stick, or answers that flow back into the void. And the reason you need to ask questions is because you need to move, metaphorically speaking. With every question you ask you get an answer, and with every answer you get you step in a direction. Your soul knows what it likes, and it will tell you 'no, that's not it', or 'hey, that's it!' when you get to the right answer!

Remember that you should not see things as you wish them to be, but as they truly are. Thus, you shouldn't get mad if you need to keep moving and head in the 'wrong' direction, but instead realise that even the 'wrong' direction has its benefits! Do you know what positive reappraisal is? Positive reappraisal is a meaning-based coping that makes you look at the good things you can get from the bad. It is the coping mechanism that restructures something stressful into something beneficial. Your relationship ended? Focus on what you learned from it. Got a bad mark in a quiz? Now you know the areas you need to improve.

It's the benefit of you knowing something you didn't know before. The benefit of turning around and going in a different direction by giving a different answer to your initial question, and thus being one step closer to your destination! Alike nutrition, a diet doesn't work the same for two different people, and that is why you must have your own answer to the question 'why?', to the question 'but why am I doing this?'. Know that, however, all roads lead to Rome, so you will get there once you get it right!

What to take away: Make sure you always have a strong reason behind what you are doing. If you do not, then you are susceptible to falling.

FOREGONE

Chapter 5A

STOP LYING TO YOURSELF

Reality denied comes back to haunt.
— PHILIP K. DICK

PURPOSE

The purpose of this chapter is to bring to attention the monster known as *lying*, and how lying to ourselves can (and will) have detrimental effects in the long run. Note that this is the 1st part, 5A, of a two-part chapter.

INTROSPECTIVE

So you've found someone you like, and they're coming over to Netflix & chill. What's your first impulse? To clean everything, obviously. You can't have your room look as bad as it looks right now, only a slob would live like this. You start by picking up your socks (masking your insecurities), your cups of coffee (straightening your banana-shape-posture), your unfolded clothes (collecting yourself), you hoover and mop (smiling and pretending your life is going great), and then take a shower to be fresh (making a persona out of this).

My question is: why isn't your room clean in the first place? Why are your walls dirty (sad thoughts), why is your doorknob damaged (trust), why is there a monster under your bed (ego)? What exactly makes you spring up to life and get to action for someone else, but not for yourself? *Why not for yourself?* Even more important, once you get comfortable with that person, say in one or two months, you do know that you'll be dropping off this fake level of intensity you have about yourself in this moment, right? It's inevitable.

It's inevitable and you know that. We talked about it before, about the balance between *the effort we make* and *the reward we get,* and that balance must always be inclined down towards the former, for nobody wants to work hard and receive almost nothing. Based on that, like a phone which is no longer new, our excitement wears off and we no longer have a reason to keep up with all the trouble that having a persona is, since we now have what we wanted and it's no longer attractive to us.

See, when we don't do things for ourselves we have no reason to keep up with what we're doing (first stage of competence). There is no apparent reward for us to keep our room clean since we've attributed the room cleaning to 'acting like a decent human being for someone else'. If you did it for yourself, your room wouldn't be dirty in the first place, right? Based on this, you know that your room will get dirty again, your cups gathered again, your clothes unwashed and thrown everywhere. To be a bit plainer and to get to the subject: why do you lie to them, and ultimately to yourself about yourself? About whom you truly are? Remember that you can't fix that which you don't know is broken!

My aim is to make sure that you don't waste your time like I did. We all lie, it happens to everyone, and most times we lie to either please a parent's wish, to defend ourselves from an abusive person, to cover up the sadness we feel about our life choices, or to hide our lack of motivation under false pretences.

It is important to rehash that we are both our employer and our employee, and that we must treat ourselves the way we would like someone else to treat us. You wouldn't like to be lied to, so why lie to someone else? To make things worse, why lie to yourself? You should question this behaviour!

'What do I hope to achieve by lying? What do I hope to avoid? Can I not achieve that which I long for without lying? Why do I lie? What makes me lie?'. These are some good questions to ponder upon.

DEFINE

What is *lying*? *Lying* is a concoction of intelligently selected words used to deceive people for a defined benefit. It is a conscious action, something people do and are aware of doing. It stems from the inability to achieve honourably what we propose to achieve. ***It is the lack of patience to learn that which we lie about.***

But why do we lie to ourselves? Maybe we lie because:

- We put our value in other people's hands since our own opinion about us brings no happiness, and as a result we engage in social activities that go against our morals in order to be a part of something, to be wanted, to feel worthy. *But why does our opinion about ourselves mean nothing?*
- We do not have the courage to realise how beautiful and short life is, and are afraid of disappointing our parents by pursuing our true passion. It's not that we want to not disappoint our parents, it's actually that we are afraid of being judged by them. *But if we know our worth and stand by our choices, why are we afraid of being judged?*
- We do not know our full potential and that we can be happy on our own, and thus we depend on toxic people that make us happy. Eventually we fall in that loop where we can't let them go because we're afraid of being miserable without them. *But why don't we know our full potential?*
- We have misled ourselves into thinking that we actually found that which we want to do whilst using *the creative process*. Because of that, we are now caught in a practice that not only we despise, but we can't continue to sustain because we aren't really driven by our true purpose, a purpose that can strengthen and push through any circumstance. How many times have we heard about people that have had a change of heart and changed their careers later in life, and how they regret not being honest with the passion they truly had in the first place? *How many years were lost?*

ILLUSTRATE

Remember the fail-safe-plans talk from this section's chapter 3? The one where my father kept asking me about my purpose? The one where I always had an answer to every question he asked?

That was me lying to myself, in more than one way: I was lying to myself that I have nothing to worry about since I'm young. I was lying to myself that I have time to find something to do. I was lying to myself that I have choices. Ultimately, *I was lying to myself about responsibility and picking it up.*

Based on this, take a second to ask yourself: 'what is there to gain from lying to myself?'. Answer truthfully before jumping to the next section.

REWARD

Complacency. Complacency is marked by self-satisfaction especially when accompanied by unawareness of the actual dangers or deficiencies.

Complacency comes before the existential crisis, which comes before the torment. Think about how comfortable it is to do nothing. I'm not talking about taking a Sunday off, or every Sunday in a month. I do that. I'm talking about lying to yourself about every little thing you do. How comfortable it is to relax knowing that 'you'll burn this XXL pizza you eat every day at the gym', or how 'you'll get a double espresso in the morning' after a night out, or anything else we lie to ourselves about that not only delays and pushes back our potential, but also hurts us by creating a habit of doing that.

You have two lives: one is given by your parents, and one is given by yourself. In the first you exist, and in the second you live, and you get control over your 2nd life only when you understand that you have no control over your 1st. What do I mean by that? I mean start playing the hand that you've been given! Start living, not only existing! Be more than your parent's child! Be your own person! I'm not asking you to be the second Einstein or Marilyn vos Savant, I'm asking you to be the first you. To see who you are, and what you can do, and you can only do that when you stop delaying your potential with your lies.

ANALYSE

'But how do we get to even realise that we're lying to ourselves?', you ask. We realise that we're lying to ourselves when we question something we're doing and realise that we're unsure of the reason behind it, but we must understand that *we have to question our behaviour in the first place*! As with everything else, if we actively pay attention to our gut feeling and let ourselves objectively guided by the *'but why?'* system, we can reach the point in our judgement that is at fault. Remember that all the problems we have are made by our choices, and in that same manner, they can be solved by our choices. Thus, when looking at our behaviour objectively, and more specifically, at the things we do that we're unsure why we do, we should ask ourselves:

- Do we really think we want to keep talking to that person that gives us negative vibes, or are we talking because we're desperate for attention and they're the only ones that provide it? *Why are we desperate for attention? (prudence)*
- Do we really think we'll burn all this daily intake of junk-food at the gym, or is this something we say because we lack control? *Why do we lack control (prudence, fortitude, and temperance)*
- Do we really think we have all the time in the world to start working on something, or are we just afraid to pick up responsibility? *Why are we afraid of responsibility? (prudence, justice, fortitude, and temperance)*.

UNDERSTAND

When you notice that you're lying to yourself, you need to truthfully question your behaviour: **'what do I hope to achieve by lying? What do I hope to avoid?'**. Whenever we lie, we do so to avoid something, be it responsibility, guilt, fault, discomfort, etc. That's it. There is no other reason why we lie.

Primarily, we lie when we are purposeless, but we also lie when we have a purpose. We lie because we are afraid to pick ourselves up and to start trying to have a better life. We lie because we lack the courage to realise that we have the power inside of us to change, to be better. We lie because it is easier to be comfortable than it is to make a change, as the ego likes to whisper.

I understand you. Trust me. I used to wake up at 5am, leave at 6am, get to work at 7am in order to prepare the shop and open by 8am, and worked until 5pm. I got home and I was tired, beaten and discouraged. But I got up, scrutinized my life by splitting it in tiny pieces, noticed and worked on correcting the smallest things first (which took as little energy as possible), made my life better by 0.5% every day or week with new habits, and worked my way towards making the bigger things straight too, and so can you!

You can get up and realise that this life is not the one you want, that even if you have a good pay and nice colleagues, that this lifestyle can't be sustained for long. That you are better than this (respectfully), and that you can change your life, one small change at a time!

'But why should I do it?', you ask. Because you only live once, and nobody will ever love you as much as you love yourself, respectfully to your mother. Nobody will listen to you and understand you as much as you will, and that should be reason enough for you to want to better yourself! Because life is poker, and you're all in! You've been given a hand, and it's time to play it as best as you can! What better purpose is there than to pursue virtues and wisdom? Than to find that which you're great at, and to give it your best every day? What better things do you have to do with your time other than to be happy?

Be rudely honest with yourself and question your life, question your state, question your future. Realise that you are allowed to be happy, and only you can make yourself happy! If others could, they'd probably activate serotonin in you and make you happy, just as you would if you could activate serotonin in other people and make them happy. But unfortunately that is not possible! We have control over our mind only, and therefore only over our choices. So start activating serotonin in yourself and start feeling worthy! Work hard for your dreams, so that you can rest well at the end of the day knowing that you did all you could! Otherwise, if you waste time and do nothing, what is going to bring you comfort and make you proud when you get in bed at the end of the day? Your height, which is defined by your genetics? Your pretty face, which you inherited? Your organs, which you can't control? Only the things you work for that you can create and influence with your choices will bring you true happiness. You got this! Never forget that!

OVERCOME

To fortify my previous statement, let's look at what *lying* is: **lying is comfort**. Lying is the banishment of one's potential in favour of the illusion of comfort. Lying is the avoidance of pain, and the soothing of ego. Lying is the addicting need to only appear great, not to be great, be it whether we lie to others or to ourselves, regardless if we lie about our possessions or our actions. As you see, lying has a lot of faces, so we must be careful because it might not be obvious sometimes that we lie to ourselves.

'So how do I find out if I'm lying to myself, and subsequently stop it?', you ask.

First of all, *you categorise your behaviour in either 'distraction/regress' or 'progress'*. As you will see in the next chapter, you will make a schedule that will help pursue your goal, say get abs for the summer. You must categorise 'crunches' as 'progress', and 'daily fast-food at late hours' as 'regress'.

Second of all, *you look at each individual action from here on out for the rest of your life, and ask yourself if that action wastes time or helps push forward your purpose*. When you're about to do something, like eating some crisps, or skipping gym, or choosing to play games instead of working, you ask yourself: 'will this action lead to progress or regress?'.

Step three, *you rinse and repeat.* 'Repetition is the mother of learning, the father of action, which makes it the architect of accomplishment', says Zig Ziglar.

What to take away: If you wish to make true progress you have to first *stop lying to yourself.* Start categorising your behaviour in 'progress' and 'distractions', and look at where your next action leads! You can either make progress or revel in distractions, but not both. Remember that just because the soul does not use words it doesn't mean that it's mute, so listen to it when you're about to engage in a behaviour. Is it 'progress' or 'regress'? Do you feel that 'push' from the soul to do it? No? Then what does it say?

FOREGONE

Chapter 5B

ADDICTION

Strength does not come from physical capacity. It comes from an indomitable will.
— MAHATMA GANDHI

PURPOSE

The purpose of the chapter is to bring in focus the subtly settled behaviours that eat away at our time and potential, and how to correct them to regain time, power, and control over our lives. This is the 2nd part, 5B, of chapter 5. Do note that I refer strictly to simple, overcomeable addictions.

INTROSPECTIVE

So you've decided you want to clean your room. As you look around in the closest level of proximity, *L1,* you start to notice your dirty socks, your cups of coffee, and your unfolded clothes. You open your eyes even wider and notice the 2nd circle of proximity, *L2.* You notice that you also haven't made your bed, hoovered, mopped, done your chores, and what else. You now start to slowly go into the 3rd circle of proximity, *L3,* and notice that your walls are dirty, your doorknob is damaged, and that there's a monster under your bed. But you only have 10 minutes every day to work on your room. What do you do? You can't fix all of that in 10 minutes, and if you had more than 10 minutes, it would take so much time to fix it all that you'd rather just lie to yourself about the state your room is in, and avoid the dauting idea of looking at the amount of work needed.

FOREGONE

This is where having a schedule comes in play. Alike a mountain, you look at the top once in order to assess what you're up against, and then you take your eyes off of the top and start focusing on every step you take. You look at the 1st circle of proximity, *L1,* the closest one to you, the one where things can be fixed in under 5 minutes, and you start fixing. One day at a time.

DEFINE

What is an *addiction*? An *addiction* is a character trait that will perfectly justify its behaviour to get its desires. Addiction is the lie we tell ourselves or someone in order to push through resistance and indulge in momentary pleasure. Addiction is the killing of our future. Ultimately, addiction is any wasted potential.

There is an old story of unknown origin that I will poorly paraphrase: 'we all have two wolves inside of us. One of them is good and one of them is bad, and every day they fight. The one that wins is the one we feed'.

In life we rarely realise that we're in the bad wolf's mouth until too late, and that's because addiction is tricky to spot since all of its wrong doings are amazingly justified by our ego. Simple, overcomeable addictions like watching tv, scrolling through social media, etc., is a great enemy to have because not only does it teach us about our intelligence and about how much of a potent negotiator we are in making up excuses and reasons to pursue something that we're addicted to, but it also shows us how adamant we can be if we truly desire something.

An addiction is powered by a seemingly indomitable answer to the question 'why?': because I need it. Simple. Elegant. Deadly! Imagine how powerful we could be if we could take control of this behaviour and use it to get addicted to the good things, like helping people, eating healthy, adopting animals, and other virtues. I jest, for no addiction is good. (temperance)

There are many forms in which this evil exists, and we can recognize it when we are tempted by it. We look at the behaviour we're about to engage in and question ourselves if this action will either lead to 'progress' or 'regress/distraction'. We fortify that by also listening to our gut feeling that says 'this is wrong, I shouldn't be doing this' and acting accordingly thereafter. Most times, unfortunately, due to fatigue and stress we shush our gut feeling away, push it into a dark room, close the door and throw the key. In doing so we feed the bad wolf.

Know that being happy takes active effort, and thus you must realise that when you're not pursuing your goals but instead give in to your addictions, you are writing cheques with your future self's potential by wasting today's time. Tomorrow there are no refunds given for today, only the guilt we have for doing some things in the past that we wouldn't do anymore today. Let that be your guide for future endeavours.

Now that we understand what it means, we must attempt to look at our own behaviour and see where we invest time poorly because of addiction. When it comes to wasting time, I like to think that you are not only yourself, but you are also *you from yesterday, today, and tomorrow*. The injury you had recently will hurt today just as much as the fast-food binging you are having this week will affect you next week. You are in a constant touch with your past and future versions simply because the lessons you learned so far help improve your current-self, and your current-self is the arrow that has been pulled back and launched into the future. You can't pull the arrow back and launch it again, but you can choose whether it's a hit or miss.

ILLUSTRATE

There is an experiment called 'The Stanford marshmallow experiment' which pertains to understanding the 'hot and cold systems' of impulsiveness. A child was offered two choices: a small and immediate reward, or a bigger but delayed reward. The experiment required the kid to remain seated at a table with a marshmallow in front of him, whilst the examiner leaves the room. The child is instructed to ring the bell if it wants to eat the marshmallow early, or to wait 15 minutes for the examiner to return and to offer the kid two marshmallows instead of one.

We all made impulse based choices in our lives, be it happy or sad ones. If you remember that emotions are *temporary* states brought on by neurophysiological changes, take a second to ask yourself: 'what is there to gain from giving in to my impulses?'. Answer truthfully before jumping to the next section.

REWARD

Obsessive risk. That is the reward.

Remember when I said that life is poker, and you're all in? I meant it. You got dealt a hand by life, and this hand is stronger than some hands, and weaker than others' hands. Regardless if you like it or not, you have to play it because it's the only one you have, and because you can win if you *choose* your battles, and that's where temperance comes in play. You must not give in to pleasures, but control them. Remember that the medicine that cures is also the medicine that kills in higher doses. If there is no serious condition (depression, disease, or anything that stops you), but instead it's just yourself and your choice of giving in to instant gratification, then please take a moment to think about your choices. Now apply that to:

- A day: you 'waste' a day watching tv. We all love a good Sunday, and I promise you unsarcastically that it is fine. I actually recommend taking Sundays off if you work 8/10 hours a day for six days straight!
- A week: you waste a week watching tv. Alright, the next time you can do this is after 4 months. Life is grind, and none is excused, so get up!
- A month: you wasted a month that will never come back. Wasted progress that could have been done, and for what? Drinks, parties, food, tv, and other activities where you impulsively agreed to join without taking a moment to think about your dreams? Get up!
- A year: don't even get me started. With one hour per day you would've been 365 hours closer to your goal. Now you're *at least* 365 hours away from your goal, and don't tell me that at least you 'made memories'. That's not the point. The point is you decided on doing something good for yourself, you decided on being noble, and you're not living up to your best. Go have one small party, one small drink, one small fast-food every Sunday, but not every day for a year. Get up!

You start obsessively risking your future because you think you have enough time, or because you feel afraid and think of yourself as unable to actually change anything. Child and dust under the rug, all over again. That's where the image from page 172 comes in play. Take it, print it, fill it, understand it. Start *living* your 2nd life, no longer only existing in the first one your parents gave you. You aren't a loser if you fall, you are a loser if you don't try to get up, and you bought this book because you don't want to stand down! *So get up!*

ANALYSE

The study showed that the kids who managed to show restraint and chose the bigger, delayed reward (delayed gratification) had overall better life outcomes than the ones who chose the smaller, instant reward (instant gratification). Upon retesting the original patients in 2011 (now in their 40's), most adults showed the same behaviour now as they did when they were a child undergoing the experiment.

The 'cold impulsive' ones who chose delayed gratification had better grades, better health, and higher education, as opposed to the 'hot impulsive' ones who chose to ring the bell and eat only a single marshmallow.

UNDERSTAND

To further fortify my point, I'd like to bring to attention how it's easy to cry over your job and colleagues, but you know what's not easy?

- To get home, to take a shower, to eat something, and to work on your future plan when you're tired.
- To decide that your life can't be what it is right now for the rest of your life, to declare that this just can't be how your life is meant to be!
- To start searching within yourself for what you like to do, to use *the creative process*, and to work two to three hours at the end of your day for yourself. For your future.
- To work when others party, when others celebrate nothing, and to get out of the hellhole that your life is.
- To be a predator, and to have a prey, a goal.

It all starts with being grateful for what you have, with charging yourself positively by appreciating that you actually have a chance to change your life. If you want to make a change you can get up and do it. You only have to focus on your goal and be grateful that you're in a position where you have good health, sustenance, a roof over your head, and time!

Unfortunately, we always strive for more power and more money, never taking a second to appreciate what we have and how miserable we would be without what we have. Our health, the health of our parents, our job, our room, these 'small' things that allow us to have a normal social life, these things without which we would be miserable, unfortunate, crippled.

OVERCOME

'Great, so how do we avoid or correct addictions?', you ask.

First of all, *you consult the previous three chapters.* Did you find something you really enjoy doing using *the creative process*? Did you find a strong answer to the question 'why do I want to do this'? Did you look at your actions and split them in 'progress' and 'distraction/regress'?

Second of all, *you now think of what choices one can take in order to better themselves.* Usually the answer to that is practice, and practice is both different and at the same time identical to each category. Be it to pick up a crayon to draw, to get a coach to teach you football, to pick up a chemistry book and to just start learning, or to engage in an apprenticeship in order to learn first-hand experience from a master, you must think of what is the first step you can take in order to better yourself. Don't know? Google 'how to be better at ....", and insert the activity you decided on in the dotted area (be it drawing, studying chemistry, etc).

Third of all, *you must make an actual schedule, preferably on a device that you carry with you, and add the practice from the previous step to the schedule.* On the next page you can see the one that I'm currently using. I split this schedule in 'mind' and 'body' time, prioritising the mind part in the first part of the day, as we use it constantly and tires faster, as opposed to the body (I write, verify, and correct about ~11 hours a day, and train two hours a day).

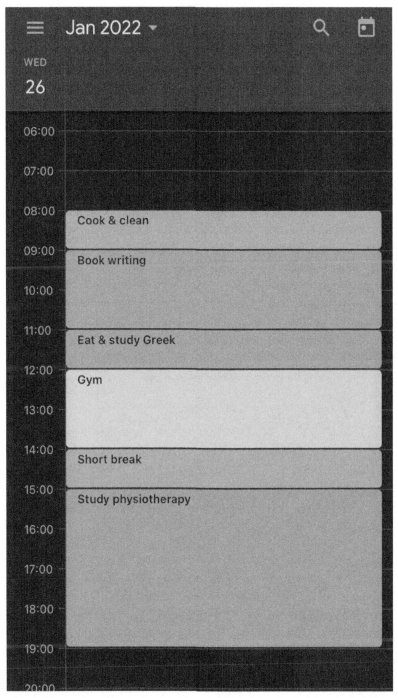

If you wish to really feel like the day isn't as daunting as it is, you can get your heaviest task out of the way in the morning. Not only is your mental state relaxed then, but overcoming a challenge generally leads to an increase in self-respect. Combine that with the contrast rule and now your day will seem like a breeze.

I also cannot stress enough the importance and effects a proper diet and sleep has on your attitude and mood. How your ability to resist temptations stems from having a strong reason for doing what you do, and is empowered by a relaxed nervous system, which is only possible with good rest, good diet, avoidance of alcohol in large quantities, avoidance of cigarettes, avoidance of stress and other negative-nervous-system-stressing-behaviours.

It is of utmost importance to have a good sleep, diet, hydration, read, laugh, and training. Without these life might seem to be pointless, as restlessness leads to poor willpower, and poor willpower leads to low quality dietary choices. A poor diet leads to a poor training which leads to a bad mood, and nobody is in the mood to laugh after having a bad day. It is a domino effect. One must make sure that not only their house is clean, but also their schedule, otherwise the tempting comfort to waste time is extremely powerful and often irresistible, and thus ensues procrastination.

What to take away: It would be great to have a schedule where you decide on your daily and weekly goals, and to stick to it daily. Not only do you eliminate addiction, but you also instil discipline and harness your true potential.

Chapter 6

THE ILLUSION OF PROGRESS

Progress is impossible without change, and those who cannot change their minds cannot change anything.
— GEORGE BERNARD SHAW

PURPOSE

Now that we've talked about finding true motivation for your goal, scheduling your tasks, and detecting and cutting addiction, we need to look at our next topic: falling in the *illusion of progress*.

INTROSPECTIVE

What is the next logical step? Urgency. Your next step is to make another schedule, but this is on a bigger scale and it serves a different purpose than the first one.

If chapter 5 was successful, then you now understand the importance of looking at your actions with the intent of putting as much value as possible in them. You now understand that chapter 5 made you split your actions in 'progress' and 'regress', and afterwards made you create a schedule that uses as much time of your day for focusing on potential, with one or two hours at the end of the day that are free for you to do as you please. Remember the cheque example: save, and then spend.

In chapter 6 we no longer worry about wasting time, for we have bigger problems: procrastination and going fast nowhere. In this chapter we will create a plan that addresses the next year(s), and separate it in short-term, medium-term, and long-term goals in order to keep track of progress, to make sure we have progress, and to make sure we also have a sense of urgency. This chapter is 'making one big appointment' with extra steps.

DEFINE

What is the *illusion of progress*? The *illusion of progress* is the act of doing something but achieving nothing. It is the act of subtly procrastinating but giving the impression that you are working hard.

'I finally got a laptop! I can now go back to working on my book! Now let's choose the cover and the font for the next 15 days. I'll worry about what the book is about later'. That right there is an example of *illusion of progress*. Although it might seem like I am productive, I am doing absolutely nothing. I could have invested those 15 days into reading about how to write a book, what a book should be made of, on key tips about making it more immersive, etc. That would have been a true progress. Instead, I have pretended that I am doing actual work out of fear of starting.

The purpose of this chapter is to show you how even having a good answer to the question 'why?' can still be insufficient. This *illusion of progress* is the base pillar of most unhappiness, and with enough time you will see how all bad things stem from it. To make things worse, it doesn't necessarily apply to wasting time with palpable things. Spending 15 days on choosing the colour to write this document with is one example, but here is a non-palpable example: choosing the easy way out.

Choosing the easy way out is the most common one we might see in life. It is that automatic consistency where you no longer think if an action has a good ending or seems to have a good ending, you just do it. Actions such as continuing university just for your parents' sake, working hard just to look like you're working hard, trying to live a life on social media that seems cool when it actually burns you out, having a good diet but ruining it every weekend.

We are all guilty of this illusion, but it is important to do something about it. For example, after facing my own *illusion of progress* and realising that I can't work with a blank page, I started writing down some issues that made my life hard, and the way I tackled them. I decided to write from the heart and to edit later in order to get some work done. As I'm writing, I start to be flooded with memories where I myself or someone I know had the *illusion of progress,* and the regret about how I myself or they could've done better. Regret and guilt are useless emotions in my opinion, but they do serve one good purpose: they tell you that you could've been better, and consequently that you know you're better than that. Let me explain with an example.

ILLUSTRATE

After securing a good bartending job that had amazing hours, a £450 per week salary, decent colleagues that I'm still friends with even today and many other benefits, I have started to slowly drift off into an *illusion of progress.* Before this job I was very disciplined with my nutrition and my training, but since we were in our early 20's and Friday noon we used to get paid, I got swayed by the entourage into a dance & dine routine where we hit the clubs, and afterwards the restaurants. I have gained an astounding amount of ten kilograms of body fat over a short period of four months. Only upon reaching Greece for my short holiday did I notice the damage I brought upon myself when I tried on my swimming shorts and realised that they needed to be combined with another pair in order to fit my new number. I satirically jest.

Based on this, take a moment to ask yourself: 'what is there to gain from not keeping track of my progress?'. Answer truthfully before jumping to the next section.

REWARD

Procrastination. This is the reward.

The reason to have a plan is because without it we can easily end up not knowing where to go. Ok, we have our goal and the plan for the day in front of us, but what determines if we've reached our goal? What achievements does it have? What marks an achievement? How do we know if we're better than yesterday? How do we know if we're moving? We need some tests.

You see, if we do not plan for the future, if we do not break our goal in small goals, each being an incrementation on the previous one, how can we know if we've reached our goal, as opposed to standing still? What do you think happens if you decide to do 30 push-ups in four months, and you do only 10 every month, without small incrementations? If your goal was 30, and after four months you do 10, that isn't progress, that's lack of progress.

ANALYSE

There have been numerous factors that should've triggered the alarm that I'm gaining weight, such as increased tiredness, opened buttons after eating, knee pain in exercises, etc. But the young mind and body cared not for that, as I had a good metabolism and an indomitable, but stupid will. I lied to myself that by doing the same kilometres every day and that by eating this much I would be able to increase my muscle mass faster, have better recovery, and other silly excuses made by my new-found pleasure. I either subconsciously realised the *illusion of progress* and covered it up with an excuse because of the *addiction* that formed, or I was really blind and ignorant.

UNDERSTAND

There are many faces the *illusion of progress* wears:

- Look at the frequently used one, *toxic positivity*, which is the kind of fake-shoulder-patting-support you receive from someone who has no care for you, only for themselves. They tell you that you're great when you're not, and you don't want to hear that. You suffer the way you are, and what you truly need is change.
- Look at all those fake online gurus that promise you millions of dollars if you just follow their free course, only to be sucked dry with sequential courses that costs thousands but achieve nothing. Scams where people make money by telling you how to make money, which is to write a book about how to make money.
- Look at those who live a fake Instagram life, they who appear to work hard only for appreciation, alike the pharisee.

- Those who are steroid-enhanced but claim to be natural, and promise you the same results if you purchase their supplements and books.
- Look at your friends who instead of helping you walk, they tell you that you should walk on that broken foot and that you don't need aid, that you are a champion!
- Look at *your addiction* and at the excuses it creates in order to 'help you feel better'.

We are surrounded by it, but do we recognize it? As you can see, the *illusion of progress* comes under many faces. It can either be wasting time, mindless consistency, fake support, etc. Whatever you do, you mustn't give in to them, for you have everything you need in your mind, and that is *planning!*

OVERCOME

You have to look at what your current goal is and to break it down in three parts: the short, medium, and long-term goal. You must look at these goals as realistically as possible. If your goal is too far-fetched and if it involves the aid of a djinn, then you might need to restructure. The only example I can think of is myself, and this is the way I declared and structured my goal:

- ***I started by declaring who I am, fundamentally***: I am a person that likes to help people. I like learning, I have learned lessons from those around me that helped better myself, and I added these lessons to the accumulated short studies I did at home on psychology and philosophy. I now feel like I am ready to give writing a chance to fulfil my fundamental desire: helping other people.
- ***I continued by declaring what I like to do***: I enjoy going to the gym and creating art. Bodybuilding is what I truly desire to pursue professionally, with art being a hobby that I do in my spare time for my own pleasure. Thus I declare that having a social media account where I could reach people would be a great idea.
- ***I then inverted the topics and I looked at what I'm not, fundamentally***: I am not willing to waste my time year after year behind a desk that pays my rent and leaves something extra for a pair of shoes or a game. This cannot be my life, and there must be

more to it. I refuse to be bounded by a continent when what I truly wish is to travel and see the world.

- *I concluded by looking at what I don't like*: being an avid beach goer and exercise enthusiast I absolutely despise not having my own brand of clothing. It would be great to have my own brand of shorts that people would also like and buy. Regarding exercise, I obviously don't mind buying supplements, but wouldn't it be better to reach that level where I can get sponsored financially and with supplements by a fitness company I desire? More passive incomes leads to more responsibility, discipline, and eventually to the long-term-goal of being able to financially sustain myself in a warmth country like Dubai every winter and spring.

Now that I have this written down it doesn't seem to be that special. It seems only a page long, but it is the sum of almost four years of searching and adding, removing and replacing, trial and error. Four years of lessons that aren't only 'done once, done for life', but they have stood the tests of time, the challenges of life, the dispute of others. I now know myself, and I'm ready to plan.

BREAK, STATE, ACT

'Great, so how do you do that?', you ask.

First of all, *you open a document, be it excel or word, or simply buy a current year calendar, and you break the year in three or four parts (break).* You need to realise that progress is like a baby: it develops itself over a steady course of time. You need to break the year in three or four parts, and realise that only with incrementations in each quarter will you improve.

Second of all, *you need to add goals to each quarter that build on the progress of the previous one (state).* Great, so you've started losing weight and writing your book. You state that the first two months are about walking 10,000 steps per day, doing 30 push-ups and abs per day, and three hours of continuous book writing. You feel that after two months pass, the same intensity will no longer promote muscle mass, and on top of that, you feel like you could push more with your book writing time. Thus, you write that the next two months you will do 60 push-ups and abs per day, 12,000 steps, and write six hours per day.

Third of all, *you need to add rewards (act).* Rewards are intrinsic and extrinsic, so you have to think of what you'll get or what you'd like to get from investing effort. The former could be better mental health, for when you look good you feel good, and the latter could be a big pizza to celebrate, with a side of red-velvet cake. You choose, mon ami! Also know that these steps apply from here-on out to all stages. Break, state, act!

Based on the goal I set, I go ahead and structure my plan using the steps above. For example, in the second month of the first year I would need to exercise and write more than what I did in the first month. So I would first write three hours a day, and then four hours a day the next month, and slowly and gradually increase to six or seven hours a day over the course of a year. I would increase gradually and realistically based on the results of the first two-three months. We don't want to over-write or over-train.

I would start the second year early on, specifically in the middle of the first year by opening a private Instagram account where I post my progress. I would take pictures of my progress and post them for six months, and when I feel confident enough I could then just turn the account public, and let people join me. Gaining followers would be my second year's purpose, and I could structure it by gaining info about marketing for the first two months, and by boosting my posts and posting weekly until the end of the second year.

I would start the third year early on, and I would start discussing the idea of a shorts company. Getting people to talk about it, discuss their opinions, whether they would be interested or not, check if there is something else they desire, etc. All of this is done by breaking the years in quarters, and planning small steps that build on the previous. Imagine if I started by saying 'I have to get 50k followers and to finish my book in one year, and above that to have my six-pack visible in three months and to reach Dubai in October 2022'. I would've been humbled and crushed instantly, and so would you if you were to have unrealistic goals. Remember that *hope is the evaluation of probability*, and there is more probability in a structured plan stretched over a longer period of years than there is in performing miracles in three months.

What to take away: Falling down isn't losing, refusing to get up is. Make a realistic short, medium, and long-term plan that tackles your true desire and pursue it, and only it. Put aside the distractions, let your entourage party and celebrate nothing every weekend whilst you focus on the vision of your successful future self and make every 4160 weeks of your life count! You only live once!

Chapter 7
DON'T COMPARE YOURSELF TO OTHERS

Be yourself; everyone else is already taken.
— OSCAR WILDE

PURPOSE

This chapter's purpose is to remind you that the valuable things in life are those that you do for yourself, and that being healthier than another doesn't stem from doing something for yourself. Note that whenever I talk about competitiveness and comparing, I refer strictly to the ego version of it.

INTROSPECTIVE

We've reached the end. The chapter that is as precious as the rest of the others. The chapter that will teach you about the importance of being healthier and better than you were yesterday for yourself, as there lies the true benefit.

Now don't get me wrong, I'm not banning competitions. Competition is great as it brings that thrill of the hunt, that purpose, that breath of life. The problem appears when we no longer engage in competitions with a challenge in mind, but with detriments: 'oh, I must be better than them, otherwise people will laugh at me. I can't lose to the scum of city, I am the best there is!'.

FOREGONE

We must only be better than others in order to beat them as equals, not to prove to ourselves that we are good, and they are not. When we aren't just anymore and laugh at another's chance to prove themselves when we beat them, or banish our effort and conclude it as a waste in comparison to another's victory is when suffering appears. What the !@#$ is even that?

DEFINE

What is *comparison*? *Comparison* is the act of putting your values against another's, and measuring the differences. It is the act of stacking your choices against another's, and seeing what you can learn. It is the action that stems from respect and friendly competitiveness. That is true comparison.

Now, a bad comparison springs from envy, usually from something that isn't noble. Why? Because your mind is envious, and the way it got to be that way is because you allowed yourself to get that way. Can't be envious if you don't consider someone's possessions as necessary, and your 'right' to possess them and deprive another of them. Think about it. Kids, adults, elders, we all have something to prove, and we never got over the 'I'll show you mine if you show me yours' logic in order to assess who's possession is bigger, and who's smaller. In order to assess who's a winner, and who's a loser. But what is good about that?

How can you sleep at night knowing that you looked at someone and said 'I'm better than you because I got this, and that', and consequently subconsciously said 'you don't have this, and that, and thus you're a loser and worth nothing'. What is better in doing this than in playing fair, in showing respect to the other for their right to try, without shaming them for their loss? As a coin has two faces, so does a situation, and just as your poker hand wins today, so too it will lose tomorrow. Now imagine you lost and read the above paragraph from the loser's point of view. Not feeling too grand, do you?

ILLUSTRATE

I've always compared myself to others. I've always tried to be better than everyone, and it always back-fired because it is a despisable behaviour. We all have someone who talks mighty about what they do and don't, and how they are great and would never do such things, God forbid. If you read this book, you know who you are.

But at a certain point, thanks to all the accumulated lessons from this book, I grew up. I simply grew up. The way you wake up one day and notice your voice changed from squeaky to pre-adult mode is the same way you wake up one day and realise that you stopped carrying about others, respectfully. You wake up alone all of a sudden, at home, with the realisation that you gained nothing from being healthier and smarter than another. Remember when I said that people are quicker to point out the wrongs of others than to clean their own room? Yeah, because the first stage of competence is a pain in the back, but boy is it a high-risk-high-reward sort of mechanism.

After I changed, people started 'including' me because I wasn't trying to prove myself anymore, but instead was just simply being me. Simply being. I didn't talk anymore to prove a point, but to ask a question. I didn't listen anymore to answer, but to understand. I didn't see things as how I want them, but as they are.

Now think about, honestly, and answer yourself truthfully before jumping to the next sub-section: 'what is there to gain from comparing myself to another in a rude way?'.

REWARD

Nothing. There is literally nothing to gain from being better than another.

But you could ask 'yeah but I can motivate myself to be better on days when I feel off, isn't that good?'. It would be if the glass was full, but the glass is empty (remember the *Prologue* chapter?). I say that the glass is empty because of two things:

- Motivation is great, but we need to be honest with ourselves: although this book seems like it can achieve the impossible, it can't. These are only words, this is just a book. The only one who can achieve the impossible is you, and even if that is the case, there will be some days where motivation won't work. No matter how strong your answer to the question 'why?' will be, you simply won't be able to motivate yourself to get up. Life happens. Based on this, my solution is to always keep consistent, disciplined. I'm currently writing this exact chapter, and I have 0 motivation to do so, but my consistency gives me power to push through! It's so easy for me to just let go of myself into the moment, and to autopilot this chapter to the end on just coffee and music. It is my reflex, my consistent trait, and thus I don't see it as a bother, even if I'm not motivated. Why? **Discipline**.

- I said that the book presumes that you are trying to be noble, so according to nobility, what is noble in trying to be better than another in a rude way? Is it good to look at another and see their goods? Are you trying to take them, or why do you look at them? Do you get energy from their misfortune?

ANALYSE

There is nothing to be gained from being better than another because you always need to do things for yourself. You must always contain your power, and not give it to others, because you can become powerless when you give them your power. Alike a house, people leave, and you become homeless when they take the power you gave them:

- If you're looking good for someone, what happens when that someone doesn't want you anymore?
- If you're studying hard for someone, ,what happens when that someone leaves your life?
- If you're being prudent for someone, what happens when that someone hurts you?

Now let's reverse that:

- If you're looking good for yourself, you can't un-want you, right?
- If you're studying hard for yourself, you can't leave you, right?
- If you're being prudent for yourself, you can't hurt you, right?

UNDERSTAND

When your doctor compares your results, he always compares your results with your previous ones. He doesn't go to Billy the athlete and says 'my God, Billy scored a perfect cholesterol again, look at that. Yours, on the other hand, is a shame'. How would you feel? Angry? Sad? Tormented? Bullied? In pain?

'Yeah but a coach always checks our results against another'. Well, duh, but he checks how you performed, not how many houses you got and how many the other doesn't. It's performance based. Sportsmanship based.

You always compare yourself with your previous-self for benefits, like better health, hygiene, peace, happiness, etc. The only reason to compare with others is for pure sportsmanship. For the thrill of the hunt. For a good laugh, a pat on the back, the respect of 'we both tried, respect to the winner, let's try better next year'. Nothing wrong with beating someone at fishing if it ends up in a handshake and a smile.

OVERCOME

'Great, so how do we stop comparing with others for the wrong reasons?', you ask.

First of all, *you question the true things to gain from doing so.* When you're home and you sit in your bed, what do you have to gain from getting angry and telling the cashier that she'll end up working there for the rest of her life, and that you drive a Chevrolet Corvette convertible? Does that bring you happiness or remorse?

Second of all, *you question what things you have to gain from comparing yourself to another.* Is there anything better in having a better cholesterol, eating more fibre carbohydrates, walking more, having better posture at your desk, and whatever else you want to be better at than another? No. What about if you compared to your past-self? Absolutely.

Third of all, *you look at the kind people in your life who made it, and see how they are still humble.* They didn't do it for others, they did it for themselves. The only person they had to prove themselves to is to themselves, for only they can bring peace and happiness in their lives with their choices. Not another. That is why they are still themselves, unchanged, helpful, kind. Because they didn't change their base character, they are still prudent, just, brave, and tempered. Iovu & Bobo, this is you guys.

What to take away: There is nothing to be won from comparing yourself to another. Do you think your suffering will evaporate from beating another? Do you think peace will be brought from being better than another? Do you think happiness will appear from rudely dominating another? No. These are creations of the self, and only appear from within, from working on one's self. I'm not saying to not fight back in self-defence, God forbid, I'm saying to not go causing trouble if you didn't get trouble.

CONCLUSION

Final chapter
BE NOBLE

The happiness of your life depends upon the quality of your thoughts: therefore, guard accordingly, and take care that you entertain no notions unsuitable to virtue and reasonable nature.
— MARCUS AURELIUS

GODSPEED

What are bad people, if not those devoid of prudence?

What is injustice, if not actions born from a lack of prudence?

What is fear, if not the failure to trust in one's prudence?

What is intemperance, if not the avoidance of one's prudence?

FOREGONE

I hope you understand now that everything *starts from within*. I hope you realise now that every action is a result of *thought*, and that thoughts are a result of judgement. I hope you realise now that judgement can be controlled by ego, and that you must find your true self. I hope you realise now that ego is formed from perception. I hope you realise now that perception is made by sensory information. I hope you realise now that sensory information doesn't always reflect reality. I hope you realise now that you do not need to have an opinion about everything. I hope you realise now that:

Those who you meet and are ignorant, envious, negligent, precipitous, inconsistent, intemperate, confused, embarrassed, gluttonous, prideful, wrathful, greedy, reckless, and timid, are only so because they are not noble. Every misery inflicted on themselves and on other people *starts from within them, from their thoughts*.

Those who are not noble and engage in bad behaviour like raising their voice, cursing, blaming, assuming, and getting angry only engage in that behaviour because *they do not define good and bad*. How can one understand, and not assume, and not get angry, and search for a solution since one does not know of which category those behaviours belong to? Since one does not know what is good and what is bad?

Those who wrong you only have power to wrong you if you are not noble and lack the understanding that everything is a thought, and a thought is a reflection of ourselves. What is an opinion, if not a reflection of self? What is the self, if not a reflection of perception? What is perception, if not the antithesis to reality? If you wouldn't let your worth be decided by external factors and realised the power within you to make a change, the power to choose to suffer less, then you'd start truly seeing that others' opinions are just a reflection of themselves, not of your true self. So when you suffer pain that is not physical, know that you suffer because of yourself and of your judgement, never because of another. The dagger of sentiment can only hurt your feelings if you stab yourself with it, for only you can put sentiment in another's words. For the same you hear a sound from a barking dog and don't let yourself unchanged, so should you hear a sound from a belittling person and don't let yourself unchanged. *You don't need to have an opinion about an opinion. You can choose to let go, to not apply context, to not apply sentiment.* Are you hurt by a spam email? Are you hurt by a conversation you don't know is happening? Things hurt when you give them context.

Those around you have not pursued you into misery, for they can only offer, not inflict. They only have control over their choice to offer you, not over your choice to accept their offer. The shame of instant gratification comes from the shame of not being tempered, from the shame of wanting to spend time with the entourage instead of investing it in removing your suffering. An entourage is not bad, a lack of temperance is. A lack of temperance that lead to choosing six hours with the entourage when two would have sufficed. When you should've invested the remaining four in your future. Do you not know that you have the skills to remove suffering, bring peace and instil happiness within you? Have I not guided you correctly? If my perception is wrong, have you not learned to research already?

'The laws that govern circumstances are abolished by new circumstances', says Napoleon Bonaparte. You must use the wisdom of others, but realise that they are only guidelines. Wisdom can't teach you the steps you must take in each specific situation, for each situation is different, but it can teach you how to walk, and that is by being noble: prudent, just, brave, and tempered.

I leave you now, for I know you are in the right hands. I thank you for taking this journey with me. I hope I didn't bore you with the wall-of-China-text, and I really wish you the best with future endeavours. As I said before, I say again: I believe in you, and since you are my equal, just as I stopped suffering so will you. Now get up, and go be noble!

O God and Heavenly Father, Grant to us the serenity of mind to accept that which cannot be changed; courage to change that which can be changed, and wisdom to know the one from the other.

Disclaimer
Last updated: February 26, 2022

Interpretation and Definitions

Interpretation

The words of which the initial letter is capitalized have meanings defined under the following conditions. The following definitions shall have the same meaning regardless of whether they appear in singular or in plural.

Definitions

For the purposes of this Disclaimer:

Company (referred to as either "the Company", "We", "Us" or "Our" in this Disclaimer) refers to FOREGONE: Know Thyself.
Service refers to the Application.
You means the individual accessing the Service, or the company, or other legal entity on behalf of which such individual is accessing or using the Service, as applicable.
Application means the software program provided by the Company downloaded by You on any electronic device named FOREGONE: Know Thyself.

Disclaimer

The information contained on the Service is for general information purposes only.

The Company assumes no responsibility for errors or omissions in the contents of the Service.

In no event shall the Company be liable for any special, direct, indirect, consequential, or incidental damages or any damages whatsoever, whether in an action of contract, negligence or other tort, arising out of or in connection with the use of the Service or the contents of the Service. The Company reserves the right to make additions, deletions, or modifications to the contents on the Service at any time without prior notice. This Disclaimer has been created with the help of the Disclaimer Template.

The Company does not warrant that the Service is free of viruses or other harmful components.

External Links Disclaimer

The Service may contain links to external websites that are not provided or maintained by or in any way affiliated with the Company.

Please note that the Company does not guarantee the accuracy, relevance, timeliness, or completeness of any information on these external websites.

Errors and Omissions Disclaimer

The information given by the Service is for general guidance on matters of interest only. Even if the Company takes every precaution to insure that the content of the Service is both current and accurate, errors can occur. Plus, given the changing nature of laws, rules and regulations, there may be delays, omissions or inaccuracies in the information contained on the Service.

The Company is not responsible for any errors or omissions, or for the results obtained from the use of this information.

Fair Use Disclaimer

The Company may use copyrighted material which has not always been specifically authorized by the copyright owner. The Company is making such material available for criticism, comment, news reporting, teaching, scholarship, or research.

The Company believes this constitutes a "fair use" of any such copyrighted material as provided for in section 107 of the United States Copyright law.

If You wish to use copyrighted material from the Service for your own purposes that go beyond fair use, You must obtain permission from the copyright owner.

Views Expressed Disclaimer

The Service may contain views and opinions which are those of the authors and do not necessarily reflect the official policy or position of any other author, agency, organization, employer or company, including the Company.

Comments published by users are their sole responsibility and the users will take full responsibility, liability and blame for any libel or litigation that results from something written in or as a direct result of something written in a comment. The Company is not liable for any comment published by users and reserves the right to delete any comment for any reason whatsoever.

No Responsibility Disclaimer

The information on the Service is provided with the understanding that the Company is not herein engaged in rendering legal, accounting, tax, or other professional advice and services. As such, it should not be used as a substitute for consultation with professional accounting, tax, legal or other competent advisers.

In no event shall the Company or its suppliers be liable for any special, incidental, indirect, or consequential damages whatsoever arising out of or in connection with your access or use or inability to access or use the Service.

"Use at Your Own Risk" Disclaimer

All information in the Service is provided "as is", with no guarantee of completeness, accuracy, timeliness or of the results obtained from the use of this information, and without warranty of any kind, express or implied, including, but not limited to warranties of performance, merchantability and fitness for a particular purpose.

The Company will not be liable to You or anyone else for any decision made or action taken in reliance on the information given by the Service or for any consequential, special or similar damages, even if advised of the possibility of such damages.

Contact Us

If you have any questions about this Disclaimer, You can contact Us:

- By email: foregoneknowthyself@yahoo.com

References

Thau, L. and Singh, P. (2020). *Anatomy, Central Nervous System.* [online] PubMed. Available at: https://www.ncbi.nlm.nih.gov/books/NBK542179/.

Bamalan, O.A. and Al Khalili, Y. (2021). *Physiology, Serotonin.* [online] PubMed. Available at: https://www.ncbi.nlm.nih.gov/books/NBK545168/.

Puig, M.V. and Gulledge, A.T. (2011). Serotonin and Prefrontal Cortex Function: Neurons, Networks, and Circuits. *Molecular Neurobiology,* [online] 44(3), pp.449–464. Available at: https://www.ncbi.nlm.nih.gov/pmc/articles/PMC3282112/.

Strüder, H.K. and Weicker, H. (2001). Physiology and Pathophysiology of the Serotonergic System and its Implications on Mental and Physical Performance. Part I. *International Journal of Sports Medicine,* 22(7), pp.467–481. Available at: https://pubmed.ncbi.nlm.nih.gov/11590474/

Bakshi, A. and Tadi, P. (2020). *Biochemistry, Serotonin.* [online] PubMed. Available at: https://www.ncbi.nlm.nih.gov/books/NBK560856/.

Sprouse-Blum, A.S., Smith, G., Sugai, D. and Parsa, F.D. (2010). Understanding endorphins and their importance in pain management. *Hawaii medical journal,* [online] 69(3), pp.70–1. Available at: https://www.ncbi.nlm.nih.gov/pmc/articles/PMC3104618/.

Watts, T.W., Duncan, G.J. and Quan, H. (2018). Revisiting the Marshmallow Test: A Conceptual Replication Investigating Links Between Early Delay of Gratification and Later Outcomes. *Psychological Science,* [online] 29(7), pp.1159–1177. Available at: https://www.ncbi.nlm.nih.gov/pmc/articles/PMC6050075/.

CLEAN YOUR ROOM - Powerful Life Advice | Jordan Peterson. [online] Available at: https://youtu.be/Vp9599kwnhM [Accessed 18 Mar. 2022]

Printed in Great Britain
by Amazon

84495390R00129